Starman

A Novel

William Lancaster

This novel is a work of fiction, and any resemblance to persons living or dead is purely coincidental.

Also by William Lancaster: *The Beast and the Cross,* a novel

Printed in the United States of America

This book is dedicated with love and gratitude to my wife, Martha Crockett Lancaster, whose love, encouragement, patience and support contributed greatly to its creation.

Contents

"It takes guts to stay married....There will be many crises between the wedding day and the golden anniversary, and the people who make it are heroes." Howard Whitman, *Philadelphia Sunday Bulletin,* January 15, 1967.

Chapter 1

Star Burst

At full throttle, Hugh Packard hit the panic bar on the door with both hands. It made a "ca-hounk" sound that resounded in the glassed foyer of Fortress Securities, Inc. The exit door vibrated against its stop. He was free, and he was elated.

The sound of traffic met his ears and the brightness of sunlight narrowed his eyes as he crossed the street to the concrete parking deck. After six years of manic manipulations of put and call options to create fortunes for himself and his clients, after six years of pounding against the conservative Fortress mind-set, after six years of trying to convince those turkeys that fortunes were at their fingertips if only they would do as he told them, this securities trader was out, through, finished.

Over the last three quarters he had beaten all sales records. During the last year alone his trading profits had topped $4,000,000. Wealthy clients willing to take high risks were pleased with the returns on their accounts. But, screw Fortress. Hugh's young ass was out of there. He walked through the parking deck toward his black, Porsche 911 Carrera convertible. The wind blew his blue suit coat open and his red tie across his shoulder. Hugh was 36 with short, dark hair, a runner's physique, and a smooth-shaven, handsome face that showed a strain underneath, like one who had seen a horror in the past that he couldn't forget.

The concrete felt like it was just below his feet and springy, as though he were walking on clear neoprene. A fear nudged at the back of his consciousness--a feeling that the concrete might just disappear and he would fall through the parking deck into unsupported space. But he dismissed that irrational fear quickly with a thought of his money. The numbers $10,140,000 appeared in his mind, the total value of his account. Plenty to support what he wanted to do. He slipped the powerful car into reverse, jerked it out of its parking space with a squeal of rubber, and sped through the exit gate using his pass card.

He barged across two lanes of traffic amid the smell of exhaust fumes and drove along the surface streets toward the interstate, changing lanes impatiently to avoid slow drivers and lines of traffic.

He accelerated down the entrance ramp as though it were a runway and broke onto the interstate in front of a Mack semi. He listened with pleasure to the quiet roar of the Porsche engine as he accelerated, watching for patrolmen. He hit 75 and found he was blocked in the first lane by a smoke-belching pick-up truck. Glancing over his shoulder and in his rear view mirror, he cut over two lanes behind a string of cars to the open third lane and pressed the accelerator until the speedometer said 80. He turned on his radar detector and cruised at this speed for a moment, settling into the pattern of traffic.

Damn slow cars in the fast lane, he said to himself, annoyed. If you're going to drive 70, get out of the fast lane. He switched right to the center lane then shot past two cars and cut them off. Traffic was heavy on this major freeway, but he reveled in the exhilaration of running the field. His cell phone rang.

"Hugh, we got your 50 June calls on Apple at your price and sold 50 June puts at the same strike price. Anything else we can do for you?"

"That's all for now, friend. Thanks."

“That might have been the last transaction for me at Fortress,” he thought, almost nostalgically. The future drew him out into its void. It would have been better, he knew, to have gotten in with another firm before he left Fortress, but that would come easily enough. He dismissed his fears.

Traffic in the center lane was slow. An impatient driver at the back of that pack switched to the fast lane right in front of Hugh. Hugh quickly braked, then shifted to the right across the center lane to an opening in the right-- like a quarterback running a broken field. He accelerated past the slow center cars, then cut left in front of them to avoid traffic coming off a ramp to his right. A driver running about the same speed as he appeared in the fast lane on his left rear fender, threatening to close off Hugh's escape route into the fast lane. Hugh accelerated to 85 and shot the gap like a motorcycle. The other driver accelerated, too, and stayed on Hugh's bumper, but Hugh sped up to widen the gap. They came upon a slow-moving Toyota in the fast lane. Hugh saw it coming first, flashed his bright lights several times in quick succession and, when the car did not move over, switched quickly to the open center lane in front of a semi. The other car was just far enough behind to have the gap close before he could follow Hugh, and he had to slow down for the Toyota or be crushed under the truck.

Gotcha, Hugh thought, hearing the blood rush through his ears.

Hugh eased back into the fast lane in front of the Toyota and edged over toward the separation wall in the median. It was a high wall one with green paddles on top. The paddles flew by in a blur, and Hugh edged over nearer the wall to heighten the exhilarating sensation of speed. He listened to the smooth roar of the engine, felt the spin of the well-balanced tires, and luxuriated in the sense of flight.

A line of cars was coming in from a ramp on the right, and in the right lane was a minivan trapped between them and an 18-wheeler in the center lane. The ramp cars barged in without yielding, and Hugh watched the panicked face of the woman driving the minivan as she tried to cut left under the rear of the big truck, catching her hood on its steel bumper. The minivan wobbled violently, then spun wildly across the center lane toward Hugh. Without flinching, Hugh cut right behind the spinning minivan and into the clear space in the center lane behind the truck. The spinning minivan crossed the fast lane and slammed into the separation wall, throwing open its mangled hood and tail gate and sending hub caps, green paddles, and car parts flying. Hugh watched the disintegrating minivan in his rear view mirror as it slid to a stop, blocking the left lane. He tried to see the driver, and he saw her put her face in her hands. Trucks and cars behind the wreck swerved and dodged to miss it in a desperate death dance. It looked to Hugh like one car rear-ended another on the other side of the minivan, but by this time he was far beyond the wreck and couldn't tell for sure.

"No use going back now," he thought. There'll be plenty of people to help and plenty of witnesses. He caught the after-smell of fear in his nostrils. "I was quick, he thought. Glad I missed it. Traffic will be tied up for a long time." The radar detector bleeped and Hugh immediately pressed the brake and slowed the speeding automobile to the limit of 65, quickly glancing around to see if he could spot the patrol car. There it was, ahead of him, coming toward him in the opposite lane, behind another car. Hugh judged he was safe. The patrolman hadn't had a clear view of him. He cruised along at what seemed like a snail's pace of 65, as innocent as an angel. Good, Hugh thought, he'll see the wreck and stop. As soon as the patrolman disappeared over a rise, Hugh accelerated until he could feel the edge of danger again, loving it.

He thought about what the managers at the office would be saying about him--not that he cared. Now we're rid of that annoyance, probably. Hugh chuckled. Let them plod along and rot with their eight per cent, he thought.

He hadn't given them much explanation about his leaving, but they knew why--they were too damned slow for him.

Hugh had set a fast pace at work. His thoughts roamed to the scene of his office. He was on the phone all the time. On his desk he had a regular phone with five lines. On his credenza beside his computer terminal he had a special phone to the Fortress options desk. On the floor under the credenza was a special phone for Maxwell Thurmond, a very big client. Over a squawk box on the right side of the credenza the New York office could alert him and all other offices when he should buy calls or puts on certain stocks. Then, he always had his cell phone. A bank of four computers followed his charts and markets. His assistants were constantly coming into his office to ask his advice on deals he had initiated which they were carrying out. His secretary moved smoothly from one task to another, getting account information for him, and she usually ate her lunch at her desk, carving out a period of stillness in the middle of the frenetic activity, a calm spot in Hugh's spinning world. It had been hard for Hugh to keep secretaries, but finally he had found one who could work methodically and still keep up the pace. Often he would work until 2:00 a.m., go home for a couple of hours sleep, and be back in the office by 7:00 a.m. Hugh had a remarkable memory for numbers, and he used it to great advantage.

He wasn't sure he understood his motivations for leaving Fortress, but he didn't require a philosophical explanation. He had been his usual fireball self these last few months, but it had required extra effort. Underneath he had sensed a black depression into which he might fall if he let his pep level down. He kept rallying himself and his staff and throwing himself against the market like a tackle sacking a quarterback, and the adrenalin had flowed to keep him going. But now he felt something lifting him out of that struggle, and he wanted to follow that feeling. It was euphoria. The Fortress organization and his fears and the threat of black depression seemed totally beneath him, and he soared in euphoric flight.

He pressed the accelerator as he shot through an empty space in the center lane. The sensation of flight sent his thoughts spinning into the future.

He himself would choose the investment firm who would have the privilege of his expertise. It would be a New York firm, and he would work in the New York office and live in Manhattan. He would carve out a power base within that firm. He would hire the best guns in the business to assist him and have a battery of secretaries to do the detail work. He would persuade all of the big Fortress clients to go with him. They would reap the harvest of Wall Street. He would be a new star in the galaxy. He would never lack for money. This was the right thing to do, he felt convinced of that.

The sound of his cell phone pulled him out of his reveries. It was the Fortress options desk at the Atlanta office again.

"Hugh, Google just raised its offer to $106 a share," said the male voice. "I thought you'd like to know that little fact."

"Hot damn!" Hugh said. "I knew that $90 offer would never stand. Whoooie! My calls will go sky high. Keep me in touch." Then he hung up.

Atlanta will find out I'm not with Fortress soon enough, he thought. Meanwhile I'll let them feed me.

Without Hugh's realizing it, the car soared to 90 miles per hour. This deal reconfirmed his dreams. He felt regal. Everything he did turned to money. He couldn't fail. His accounts would all make big profits, too, and that would only help him persuade them to go with him to the new firm he would choose. Fortress would suffer from the loss, but they would just have to do without them. He was glad to be free from Fortress. Those slow bastards would never make any money, he thought. They didn't want to take any risks. They weren't aggressive. All they knew was value investing. Look at fundamentals. Look at corporate profits. Look at dividends. Buy treasury bonds, he thought contemptuously. That was the slow way. That was the way to keep a fortune, but not to make one. They never really dreamed the American dream. They had no gigantic vision. They had never been captivated by the towering canyons of Manhattan nor caught the vision of the fortunes that lay behind that splendor. But he had.

He had grown up near New York City. He had ridden the trains to downtown Manhattan and walked among the giants of those fabulous streets. He had stridden by the uniformed doormen of Park Avenue apartments. He had ridden the Staten Island Ferry and seen the massive, magic city floating Disney-like upon the burnished, silver-blue harbor. He had heard the stories of the men who had built her. As a youth he had invaded that island completely with a plan to capture it, but its wealth had been overpowering for him, and instead he had been captured by the infectious American dream of which the island is a carrier.

The Fortress managers did not have that dream, did not want to soar, he thought. They did not have the ambition to drink from that fountain. They could not think outside the box, could not break the unbroken. So, leave them behind. Drop them. Resign. Cut them off. He knew he could do better. If they wouldn't listen to him, they could do without him. They were just a bunch of tightwad bankers, and he felt contempt for them.

His thoughts turned to Margo, and he felt a surge of desire. He had called Margo from his office to tell her he wanted to see her, and she had told him to come by. But she wouldn't be home for another half hour. He headed for a mall near her condominium where he could kill some time. He could use some new clothes. He went to Brooks Brothers and bought a sport coat, seven expensive knit shirts, a fabric belt with yachts on it, three pairs of lightweight slacks, two bathing suits, a pair of pajamas, and some deck shoes, white socks and boxer shorts. As he was leaving the store, a leather suitcase and a matching shaving kit in the window caught his eye, and he went back in and bought these too, putting it all on his American Express Card. He put the bags with his other purchases inside the suitcase, and marched out down the mall.

He thought he saw Margo walking toward him, but it was another woman. Margo was beautiful and exciting, younger than Hugh, with light brown hair and smooth skin. He dwelled on the thoughts of her. She had attracted him right away with her firm, no nonsense approach to life. She was a career woman who had earned her degree in economics. She worked with an accounting firm as a consultant to large corporations. She had never married, though she had had a series of serious boyfriends. He had met her at a seminar on the economic outlook for the year ahead. He remembered the first sight he had had of her. She had been eating a doughnut, a cup of Starbucks mocha in her hand, standing by herself during a break. He saw again the sensuous image of her lips caressing the doughnut, her eyes catching his, her enticing figure. She had been wearing a tweed suit with a pale yellow knit top under the coat, and her breasts lifted up between the lapels in a most attractive way. His thoughts of her made him feel high. He was anxious to see her.

He left the mall at 6:00 and headed for her condo. Margo's car was there. Without knocking, he opened her door and walked in, inhaling the sweet smell of woman.

"Hi!" he called.

"I'm in here," she called from the bedroom. She was pulling a pair of white shorts over her low-cut panties when he went in.

"Hello, Sweets," he said, putting his arms around her bare waist and kissing her.

"What's this all about?" she asked.

"I quit Fortress."

"That's it? You just quit?"

"Yeah, I'm through with those turkeys, and I feel great! I'm free! I'm soaring!"

She looked at him inquisitively, then pulled on a mauve knit top over her bare breasts.

"Hey, it's all right. It's fine. I've got money. We can do things, go places!"

He put his arms around her and kissed her.

"I'd better get supper," she said. "I'm starved and I've got some work to do tonight." She walked from the bedroom through the white, high-ceiling living area into the kitchen. Margo's condominium spoke of modern elegance. The walls and carpet were grayish white. The rounded, stuffed sofa and chairs were white, and large, round, white lamps stood on two glass-topped end tables. A glass cocktail table sat in front of the sofa. The ceiling rose at an angle and shot up above a balcony which overlooked the living area. Tall, green, thin-leafed plants stood in strategic places. A gleaming, black laptop occupied a shiny wooden table in a spare bedroom. Everything looked light, clean and new.

"You brought work home again? Can't you put it off? I want you!" Hugh said.

"Not this. It's just too important. Listen, why don't you get a drink. Settle down."

"Hell, no! I don't want to settle down," Hugh burst out suddenly. "I feel good! Don't you understand!" he said.

"Not really. I don't know what's gotten into you, but I think you'd better get hold of yourself."

"I'm going to move to a big firm. I'm going to build an empire. I don't need those people."

"Well, I don't need you flying around here like a hot air balloon. I've got a career! I can't go running off with you all day and all night."

"Can't you just let up for one night!" he said. "I make the biggest move of my life and you can't even stop for one night to celebrate with me."

Anger was dissolving Hugh's euphoria. He had to get out fast.

"Look, I'll see you another time," he said, walking to the door. She came over, turned him around gently, and kissed him. "Call me?" she said. "So I'll know you're all right?"

"Okay."

Hugh closed the door. So, she was in a bad mood, he thought. So, that doesn't change anything. I'm still free. He walked out and inhaled the moist night air. In his Porsche, he pressed the accelerator, pushing the tachometer toward the red line, then leveled off at 45 for a traffic light. I'll have to lie to Anne, he thought.

Anne, his wife, would be at home. She would be fixing supper for the girls and she would keep some food warm for him. That was the routine. She was accustomed to his late hours. He thought about her, bending over the kitchen table with plates of food, the light over the table adding yellow warmth to her face as she fed their two children. Somehow, he didn't feel a part of that scene. If his encounter with Margo had dulled his enthusiasm, his thoughts of seeing Anne dissolved it. He sensed the black chasm of depression coming up toward him.

"I'm home," he said as he walked in the back door. The savory smell of hot food greeted him.

"Hello, Dear," Anne said as she came over to him and gave him a kiss. "You tired?"

"Yea," he said. "It's been a long day."

"The work on the new accounts going okay?"

"Yea, okay. Still got a lot to do. What's for supper?"

"Fried chicken, asparagus, black eyed peas..." she said.

"Sounds good. I'm hungry."

He stood by the stove and watched her put food on their plates. Her hips and waist had widened after the birth of their two girls. She was tall, though, and firm, and still carried herself with poise. Her face was rounded by her honey blond hair that curved over her ears and fell neatly to her shoulders. Her eyebrows were blond, too, and gave her face a soft appearance. Her voice was smooth and caring, and seemed to quiver as she tentatively felt out his mood. She was a southern woman, and at 34, after nine years of marriage, she had acquired a pleasant mellowness.

She put the two plates on the table and gently sat down with him.

Angie came in. She was the younger of the two girls--two and a half. She wrapped one arm around Hugh's thigh and hugged it.

"Hi, Daddy," she said.

"Hi, Hon," he said and stroked her back with his left hand. "You doin' all right?"

Without speaking, Angie pushed off his thigh and went into the den where she sat on the floor with a picture book in front of the television.

Anne and Hugh ate quietly with only light conversation to dispel the silence. The hanging light fixture over the table cast its glow over the couple as though it were trying to warm up their relationship.

"This is good chicken."

"I got it at La Boucherie, that new meat shop."

"It's good."

"Elizabeth brought home a note from her teacher today. She said Elizabeth had done very well on her math and she wanted us to know about it. She seemed very pleased."

"That's good."

After supper, Hugh went into the den to read the paper. Anne cleaned the kitchen, then helped the children into bed. Hugh held the paper in front of him, but he wasn't reading. He was thinking about what he would do. He didn't feel euphoric anymore like he did when he banged out the door at Fortress. He felt bored. He wanted to get that good feeling back. He knew what he would do. He would leave in the morning, just like he was going to the office, only he would be leaving. No hassles. He had the suitcase of new clothes in the Porsche. He could buy others. He would go. Just go. And, in the morning, he did.

Chapter 2

Shooting Star

Anne didn't learn that Hugh was gone until the next night. He was later than usual coming home, so Anne called his cell phone. No answer. Voice mail. Then she called Hugh's secretary at home.

"Hugh hasn't come home yet. Do you know where he is?"

"No, I don't. He didn't come by the office today."

"He didn't come to the office? Where was he?"

There was an awkward silence.

"You know he quit, don't you."

"No, when?"

"Yesterday. All of a sudden."

"No...."

"Yes, he told the managers he was leaving. He didn't really tell any of us why, but he seemed real happy about it. I thought you knew."

"No. He's not here. Where could he be?"

"I don't know."

Another silence.

"Well, thanks for telling me...."

"I'm sorry to be the one. If I can help..."

"Yea. I'll let you know."

Anne hung up the phone, sat down, put her hand against her mouth, and pondered. What could be going on with Hugh? What could have happened? Why didn't he tell me? No explanation came. She suppressed her fear and went into the den.

"Time for bed, girls," she said.

"Mo-om."

"No complaining, now, it's bath time."

Anne put the girls through their bedtime routine and kissed them good night. Then she went into the couple's bedroom and looked for clues, a note, anything. Hugh's clothes were all there. Everything looked normal. He would be home, she thought. He was just late. She bathed and put on her nightgown. In bed staring at the dark ceiling, she listened to the silence of the night, hanging on every sound, hoping to hear Hugh. Finally, she dropped off to sleep.

The next morning Hugh awoke and remembered where he was--the Holiday Inn on I-95 headed south. It was 7:05 a.m. He felt good again. He showered and shaved and went down for breakfast in the restaurant. Then he put his things in the new suitcase and checked out of the motel, putting the charges on a credit card.

On the interstate, he had a hard time keeping the Porsche down to the speed limit, and finally he quit trying and let the car have its head. He felt great. The sun was shining. Being on the road gave him a feeling of liberation and independence. New worlds in which he had no responsibilities except for himself lay before him. Everything seemed fresh and new. He swept past whole cities, eyeing them with a traveler's detachment, as though all the life-struggles of all the people who populated those glimmering towers and heat-shimmering streets were there simply to satisfy his appetite for visual delight. Cars flickered past, each one carrying with it the diamond-sparkled freshness of this new era that rolled into his view as though on a panoramic movie screen while the wheels of his magical car turned the road beneath him like a fast river. He was moving, going, doing, running, and it felt like accomplishment. He was high.

He put a CD into the slot--Pachelbel's "Canon in D" with other Baroque favorites. The music was soothing and sounded more beautiful than he had ever heard it before. He tapped the steering wheel with his fingers to the slow count of the music. Traffic thickened near Jacksonville, and he sped through, changing lanes easily to pick the fastest route. He raced across the St. John's River Bridge and looked down at the broad expanse of water with the morning sun shimmering on it. A tug boat plowed upstream. A large sailboat plunged seaward under bright colored spinnaker. I'd love to be out there, he thought.

He stopped at a McDonald's for lunch, and eating inside at a table alone, he had a strange sensation. He looked around at the other people in the restaurant as though he were noticing them as human beings for the first time. It was as though they were all on an elevator that became stuck, and suddenly the cool, impersonal, formal, non-relationships that people practice in public seemed broken down, and they needed each other. He imagined they would actually talk, actually share something of themselves and their talents and histories. In his vision, he thought he knew them already.

A young woman sat alone at a table. She had long, straight blond hair the texture of an afghan hound's that fell straight and strawy down her back to her waist. Hugh couldn't see her face for her hair. A dark young man came with food and sat with her. When they stood to leave, the dark man took her elbows and kissed her lightly on the lips, a public voucher of love. Dearly beloved, we are assembled here in the presence of God, to join this man and this woman... Hugh remembered the phrase from the marriage service. Three young, stout men sat at a table. One rested his foot on a chair, good old boys talking over the day's work. A woman with two small children ate next to a man who could have been her husband, except he was sitting at a separate table. Two working women discussed their office. A group of landscapers huddled at a table.

In Hugh's mind, they all began to talk to one another, greet each other cordially, tell something of their life's most pressing concerns. He stood up to leave, and the vision vanished, and they all became mere advertisements of people.

He pressed on through the afternoon down I-95 south until he came to Fort Lauderdale. He arrived late and checked into a motel, tired.

Anne awoke and turned toward the other side of the bed. No Hugh. With her hand she felt the empty space below the pillow as though to make sure he really wasn't there. Her lips tightened. She got out of bed, put on her robe and went to the kitchen where she began preparing breakfast. Elizabeth came in sleepy-eyed.

"Where's Daddy?" she asked.

Anne thought before she answered. "He had to go on a business trip," she said.

"Why is Daddy away so much?" Elizabeth asked.

"It's part of his job," Anne said.

Anne aroused Angie and fed and dressed both girls, trying to be cheerful and positive. Then she took Elizabeth to school and Angie to the church's child development center. On the way back, she decided to stop at her friend Sally's house. She didn't call before going, because she and Sally often got together in the mornings to drink coffee and talk. She parked the car in front of the two-story colonial.

Sally was a plain but warm and cheerful person. Wholesome was a word that fit Sally. She was a Midwesterner with a refreshing openness toward other people. The two women were close to the same age, and both had young children. Sally, dressed in a pink jogging suit, swung open the door and welcomed her friend with a cheerful smile. She led Anne into the kitchen where the aroma of breakfast still lingered in the air.

"I don't know where Hugh is," Anne finally said over a cup of decaffeinated coffee.

"What do you mean?" Sally asked.

"I mean, I think he's gone."

"Oh, Anne... You mean he's left you?" Sally's face showed shock.

"I think so. He quit his job at Fortress without telling me, and yesterday he didn't come home, and I haven't seen or heard from him since."

"Oh, Anne...How awful!"

Anne fought back tears. "I kept thinking he would come home, but he hasn't. It's been 30 hours since he left. I don't know what to do. Should I call the police?"

"What did they say at Fortress?"

"They said he just left. He just went in and resigned. They said he felt happy about it."

"It doesn't sound like he's been kidnapped or anything. I don't think I would call the police. What happened? Was he having problems?"

"He's been working awfully hard. There are always crises at work, but he seemed to be handling them all right. He worked long hours, but he thrived on it. I don't know."

"What about at home? Was everything all right?"

"I thought so. Hugh has always kept his feelings to himself, but I didn't notice anything unusual. He seemed to be all right, but he didn't talk much. I just don't know."

"Have you called his mother?"

"No. I didn't want to upset her. This will really tear her up."

"Maybe you better call. She might know something, have some idea."

"Okay."

"Oh, Anne, I just hurt for you!"

Anne started to cry and Sally got her a tissue. She patted Anne on the back and gave her an awkward hug as she sat at the kitchen table.

"What do the girls know?" Sally asked.

"I told them he was away on business. I didn't know what to say."

"He'll show up. I don't think Hugh would just leave forever. Maybe he will call."

"I hope so. This is awful. If I just had some idea where he was. If I just knew he was all right. If I could just punch him in the damn nose!" Anne said and laughed through her tears.

Sally laughed too. "I know how you feel. I'd like to punch him in the nose too. Oh, Anne..." she hugged her again.

"Come eat supper with us tonight," Sally said.

"I don't know. I don't want to leave the girls."

"You need some time for you, too."

"Hugh might call."

"Why are you worried about him? He's not worried about you! He'll reach you."

"Okay. I'll try to get a sitter. What time should I come?"

"Oh, anytime. Come about six and we can have a drink and talk."

Anne spent the rest of the day waiting for her phone to ring. She went out briefly to pick up the girls and buy some milk and bread and bananas. It was hard for her to clean the house. She was depressed.

She decided to call Hugh's mother in New York. Mrs. Packard was frail at 74. She had lived a life of lonely struggle raising her two sons without a husband. They were everything to her. If anything, she had leaned on them too hard for emotional support, and now they both found it difficult to be near her. Nonetheless, they were her life's accomplishment. Their achievements were her achievements, their successes her successes. Having worked low paying jobs all her adult life, they were all she had to show for her years of effort. She would take Hugh's disappearance hard.

"Hugh is too much like his father," Mrs. Packard said in response to the dreary news.

The cold phrase echoed in Anne's mind afterwards. What was Hugh's father like? He had always been a mystery to Hugh and even more so to Anne, one of those topics families skirt in conversation. Mrs. Packard knew more, but the subject was too painful for her to review.

Her phrase aroused a fear in Anne that the black mystery surrounding Hugh's father might envelop him, too, now, and take him from her life.

That night Anne had supper with Sally and her husband, Ken. Ken was successful, like Hugh, but so different from Hugh. He was tall with a country handsomeness and a football player's build. He had curly blond hair and a square jaw with a cleavage in it. Unlike Hugh, Ken had an air of comfortable security about him. Ken was president of his family's furniture manufacturing company. His father had passed retirement age and, while he still kept his hand in the company, he left it to Ken to run.

With Ken, you felt as though you were at a family beach house that had been handed down through generations, that spoke of old wealth, that made you feel safe in the informal warmth of straw rugs and sand-scuffed wooden floors and white curtains in breeze-filled windows and comfortable sofas and bourbon and water on ice. Ken gave you the relaxed impression he had just come from football practice where he was the captain of the team. He had a simple, unsophisticated approach to life. Where Hugh's success resulted from his anxious drive, Ken's seemed to come without effort. Ken and Sally's relationship with each other was natural and without strain. Their actions and conversations folded into one another like dough folded into itself.

Their house had a well-appointed living room and dining room, but the large, warm den was where life focused for them and their three children. The kitchen was large, and had room for a six-place table at which most meals were eaten.

"I can't understand Hugh," Ken said as the three of them were eating at the table. The children had eaten earlier and were in the den. "How could he disappear without a word? That's very strange." Ken sounded indignant. "It just doesn't seem like him. You mean he didn't even leave a note? He didn't say anything? Did you notice anything different about him? Anything strange?"

"No, nothing very different," Anne said. "I did notice that when we played bridge with the Hansens a couple of weeks ago, Hugh didn't seem to be himself. He didn't play well. He couldn't keep his attention on the game. He was slow playing his cards. It took him a long time to make bids, and I wondered if one of his moods was starting."

"Did Hugh have bad moods?" Sally asked.

"Yes. You wouldn't have noticed it because he never let on, but every once in a while he would start drinking more and become sullen and...depressed. After a while I learned to tell when one of these moods was coming on, and I could brace myself for it."

"I never noticed that," Ken said. "Did this happen often?"

"Maybe once a year, more or less. He would just lose interest in things. He wouldn't have much energy. He wouldn't be very enthusiastic about his work and he just wanted to mope around and be by himself. He's not very pleasant to be around when he's like that. But most of the time he's very upbeat and outgoing and enthusiastic."

"He always seemed to be pretty happy to me," Sally said.

"I wouldn't call him happy," Anne said, "but I know what you mean. He's too ambitious to be happy. He's never satisfied with what he has. He's restless and always wants more. He stays on top of things, but he's driven, as though something were chasing him, as though a hungry tiger were right behind him. He's always that way, no matter how much we have. I think it's because of his family background.

"One thing about Hugh, he never, ever wants to be poor. I think he would just as soon be dead. His family had such a financial struggle when he was growing up, he decided when he was young that he would not live like that. I think he would do almost anything to avoid it. His whole life seems to focus on making money. He will pay a little attention to the children and me when he's home, but always in the back of his mind the wheels are turning about ways he can make money."

"I've noticed he never seems to talk about you and the children. He only wants to talk about business," Sally said.

"Yea, he's always asking me about the furniture business, or real estate," Ken said. "You can tell he's always probing for profitable investments. I guess that's why he's so successful."

"It's bothered me," Sally said. "He has a beautiful wife and two lovely daughters, but he hardly knows you exist."

"But I know he thinks about us a lot," Anne said. "In many ways, we have a good life. He's always coming home with something new for the house. He bought Elizabeth an iPad so she can play games on it and learn how to work it."

"Yes," Sally said, "but that's not love. That's just his materialism. He gets those things for himself as much as for you and the children."

"Maybe so," Anne said. "But he's not hard-hearted or anything." Her voice rose in defense of her husband. "He really is a very nice guy, very kind, even, sometimes."

"Well, Hugh can be quite pleasant to be around," Sally said. "He can be very charming, in fact. Did you call his mother?"

"Yes."

"What did she say?"

"She sounded very disappointed. But she has no idea where he might be."

"I had hoped she might."

"She doesn't know anything."

"I just hope he shows up soon. I know it must be agony for you not knowing where he is."

"Yea, it's pretty bad." Anne sounded reflective.

"Did you know the Arringtons have been going through a hellacious time?" Sally asked.

"I'm afraid I've lost touch with them," Anne said.

"Trot is living in an apartment, and Marilyn is in the house. The kids are with her, but Trot wants joint custody. They're at war and they're both hurting a lot."

"I never knew what happened to them. All of a sudden they were just separated," Anne said.

"Trot left her and the children. They had problems for a long time, but Marilyn thought they could work them out. Apparently they couldn't."

"I never even realized they were having problems," Anne said. "I never got to know Trot very well. He joked around a lot, but he always seemed angry."

"I noticed that too," Sally said. "There was an edge to his humor. You might think he was being jovial and friendly, but his humor tended to be a put down toward others. I think a lot of it was directed at Marilyn."

"That's too bad," Ken said. "Marilyn's a good looking woman. I've always thought her face looked like the Venus de Milo, and she has that long, pretty, brown hair she wears in a braid down her back."

"Of course, Marilyn has her faults, too," Sally said. "She can be stubborn and insist on her own way a lot. She is always maneuvering for something she wants."

"Why did they break up?" Anne asked.

"Trot was having an affair. It was with a woman who worked at the office. Marilyn found out about it and was really hurt and angry. She tried to get Trot to break it off, but he didn't want to. So, she told him she had had an affair years ago. He flew off the handle. He just couldn't take it."

"Good heavens! When did she have an affair?" Anne asked.

"It was about four years after they were married, while Trot was getting his contracting business established. Marilyn met this man at the club where she played tennis. Trot was spending so much time at the office that Marilyn was by herself a lot. She was lonely and vulnerable. This guy came along, and pretty soon they were in bed. But Marilyn broke it off after a while and never told Trot--until she found out about his affair."

"What a mess."

"Yes. It's been awfully painful. Trot is still seeing the other woman, Marilyn says. She wanted to forgive and forget and work it out, but Trot apparently was too attached to this woman to break it off. He refused to go to counseling with her."

"That's really sad. How is Marilyn doing?"

"She's been awfully depressed. I worried about her for a while, especially right after Trot left her. She came over here often and we talked. She was so depressed at first she couldn't look after the children. She went to her parents' home and stayed a few weeks with the kids. Her mother was really good for all of them. Her doctor put her on an antidepressant, and that helped.

"Trot was very angry with her and even hit her once before he left. He told her he wanted her out of his life forever. Then he cut off communication with her. He wouldn't answer when she called on the cell phone and wouldn't respond when she tried to email. He retreated behind a wall of silence. That was worse than hitting her. They communicate through their lawyers.

"She felt horribly guilty about the affair she had had. She blamed herself for destroying the marriage. That didn't help the depression. She played that game, 'If only I had...' you know? And she was pretty hard on herself."

After supper, Anne drove home and parked the car in the driveway. She closed the car door, leaned against it and tilted her head back with her eyes closed. When she opened them, her eyes focused on the night sky spread high above her. Hugh is somewhere under those same stars, she thought. But where? The stars were so clear, so silent. She gazed at them. They seemed to move toward her, burning tiny unseen pathways through the vapid darkness. Then they appeared to stop, burning little holes in the vast retina of the black universe, burning their images onto the retinas of her eyes. A streak of light drew itself across the sky. Right where she was looking--a shooting star. It, too, burned its image into her. She felt dizzy. She looked at her hands. They were grey in the darkness. They seemed so far away, as though they belonged to someone else. She felt alone. She began to cry. Then she turned and walked toward her house and her waiting children.

Chapter 3

Star Bright

Refreshed by the night's rest, Hugh left the Fort Lauderdale motel to eat some breakfast at a restaurant and to get his bearings. He felt an urge to go toward the ocean, to breathe deeply of its salt smell, to see the sharp, thin line of the horizon and know by its proximity his orientation on the planet. He wanted to feel heat rising from the sand and catch a whiff of sun tan lotion carried on the breeze from a sensuous, bronzed, bikini-clad body.

So, after breakfast, he went to the beach, to a place he had frequented in carefree times when crowds of youthful students had unleashed their pent-up sensuality into the warm sea breeze. The beach seemed nearly deserted in the still, morning coolness with only a few beachcombers in shorts walking the ruffled line of shells near the water. The visions he held in his head of spring break crowds vanished before the reality of the nearly empty place. Looking up and down the stretch of cool, seaweed-littered sand and ice-green water, he saw and heard the sound of a breaker clapping its water closed on itself, an empty pop like the calling of a ghost drowned long ago in the sea. Chilled and disappointed, he left.

Back at the motel, he searched the internet and called a real estate agent. "I'm in the market for a condominium, something on the water with a dock," he said.

In a whirlwind of talk and activity, a hyper real estate agent who always left his car engine running showed him three. Hugh came back to one on a canal that led into the Intracoastal Waterway.

Seen from a distance, this condominium complex had the character of a street full of tall, narrow European buildings. In fact, the complex did contain a marina store, a restaurant, a yacht broker, and several small shops in addition to the residential units. The buildings included about 40 condominiums built in the coastal style with a utility area on the ground and two stories of living area above. Angled gabled roofs, dormers, chimneys and balconies made them most attractive to look at and defeated the monotony inherent in most complexes. The buildings faced the canal where floating docks rose and fell with the tide. Concrete piling pinned the docks in place above the muddy bottom. Beyond the docks and the canal were beautiful lawns and houses on the other side.

The place was ideal for Hugh. The unit he chose, one on the end of a building, with windows on three sides and a balcony on two, was very expensive, but that only made it more attractive to Hugh. He rationalized the extravagant purchase as an investment. The condominium would appreciate in value, he thought, and would be a vacation place to which he could escape when he felt very high or very low. The condominium would give him a place to take a warm break from the harsh New York winter--once he became established there. The purchase fulfilled in him a long-standing desire to have a dwelling place at Fort Lauderdale.

The unit had been furnished by the previous owner, and Hugh bought it furniture and all. Hugh arranged to rent the condominium until he could close on it.

Hugh picked up his cell phone and called a securities trader at Fortress with whom he had made an arrangement to make trades on his account when he was away from the office.

"Richard? This is Hugh Packard. I want you to sell some stock out of my account."

"No problem, Hugh. Right now the Dow is up 53 on volume of 84 million shares and gainers are outpacing losers by three to two. What do you want to sell?"

"Sell all the Apple and the Amazon and the Microsoft."

There was a pause as the broker called up Hugh's account on the computer.

"Sell 1,200 shares of Apple and 1,000 of Amazon and 1,000 of Microsoft. Okay. What else?"

"I want you to wire $450,000 into my bank account."

"You want to give me that in writing?"

"Just wire it, and I'll send you an email."

"Okay, Hugh."

Hugh gave him his new address.

"What are you up to in Florida?" Richard asked.

"I'm setting up a new base of operations, Richard. I'm going in with a big New York brokerage firm, and I want you to be in on it. None of this Mickey Mouse stuff like Fortress, we're going to play the options market and make some big money. I'll let you know when the time comes, but it's going to be big, the opportunity of a lifetime, and I'm going to make sure there's a place in it for you. Just hold on for now, though, and I'll be in touch. And, Richard, wire that money today."

"Will do, Hugh. You keep me in touch, though, about this new deal."

"You got it," Hugh said, then hung up feeling exhilarated. He loved making deals, and buying and selling stock excited him, especially when he could make a solid profit as he would on the Apple and Amazon and Microsoft. He stretched his arms back over his head as he walked along the docks toward his condominium, satisfied that the money for the unit would be on the way. The funds would give him some to live on, too.

Hugh thought about Anne. She would be frantic. He would call her--later. First, he needed to buy a new cell phone and find a supermarket. He found an Apple store and bought the latest iPhone. Then he drove to the nearest shopping area and found a supermarket. When he came back and got out of the Porsche with one of the bags of food, a young woman in a straight black dress and bare legs was getting out of her car, also carrying a bag of groceries. Hugh noticed the flash of leg as she got out of the car and bent over to pick up her groceries.

"Must be the time to stock up on food," Hugh said to her.

"Must be," she said. "Eating is a habit I haven't been able to break."

"And not one I want to break. It sure takes a lot of food to stock a kitchen."

"You just moving in?"

"Just today."

"My name's Brenda Jacobs," she said, extending her right hand while hugging a paper bag of groceries. Brenda was about 30 and had dark brown hair pulled back in a clasp. She had dark eyebrows over clear, intelligent brown eyes.

"I'm Hugh Packard."

"I live right there," she said, pointing to a nearby unit. "We'll have to get together for a drink or something." "Sounds good to me," Hugh said, "How about 5:30?"

"Well, okay," she said, and added, "you don't waste any time, do you?"

"Time's too precious to waste," Hugh said with mock pomposity.

He finished bringing in the groceries, making three trips to the car. He kept thinking over and over, "I have to call Anne," but he didn't want to do it. He forced himself to pick up his old cell phone and call his home number. On the third ring, Anne answered.

"Hello."

"Anne, it's me."

"Hugh! Where are you?"

"I'm in Florida."

"Florida! What are you doing in Florida? What's going on?"

"Anne, I just need a little time to think some things over."

"What do you mean?"

"I just have to work some things out for myself," Hugh said.

"Hugh, you quit your job. You left without even telling me. Do you know what you are doing to us?"

"I know, Anne, but I just have to have some time to myself."

Anne felt angry. She wanted to say, "You bastard! What the hell are you doing? Do you know what you're doing to me and the girls? What's gotten into you?" But she couldn't. She was afraid she might drive him farther away. Instead, she started crying.

"I don't understand, Hugh. I thought everything was all right."

"A lot's been happening that you don't know about."

"What do you mean?" Anne asked.

"Look, this is not the time to talk about it. I'll stay in touch."

"Hugh, we have to talk."

"Not now. I'll call you."

"What'll I tell the girls?"

"Tell them I'll be away for a while."

"Hugh, you can't do this."

"Look, I gotta go now."

"How can I reach you?"

"I said I'd stay in touch."

"Come home, Hugh, please."

"No. Not now. Maybe later. Give me a little time. I gotta go. I'll talk to you later."

"Hugh..."

"Bye."

Anne hung up the phone and cried. Hugh really had left. She couldn't believe it. She felt dizzy and sick. Is this actually happening? she asked herself. She felt depressed. She went to the door to the den and looked in at the girls quietly playing. Then she went to her room. She felt as though someone had thrown a black net over her, trapping her under its web.

Hugh hung up the phone and sighed. He felt bad about it, but he had to do it. An angry gloom fell over him. He went to the refrigerator, took out a beer and opened it with a pfitzs sound.

He looked at his watch. It was almost 5:30. He hadn't told Brenda where they would meet, so, leaving the beer, he went to her door and knocked. She came, still wearing her black dress, but her hair was now loose around her shoulders.

"Come over to my place, we'll have that drink."

"Okay. Let me get my keys." She disappeared into the condo and came back in a moment with a handful of keys on a large, jingling key ring.

"So, where you from?" Hugh asked her over a drink.

"Right here in Fort Lauderdale."

"You mean you've lived here all your life?"

"Grew up right here. Never lived anywhere else, except in college."

"Where'd you go to college?"

"Tallahassee."

"I used to come here on spring breaks when I was in college," Hugh said.

"Oh, yeah? That's a mob scene. But a lot of fun."

"I guess if you lived here it was different."

"Yea, but we used to have a good time, too. Actually, the good time lasted all summer long if you lived here. People came from all over to spend a week or two, then they went back to wherever they're from. They could be a lot of fun. No ties, no commitments. Just have a good time."

Brenda took a drink. "So, where're you from and what do you do?" she asked.

"I'm a New York investment trader," he lied.

"Why you buying a condo here?"

"It's just a get-a-way place. It's an investment. I'll spend part of my time here and the rest in New York. I'm going to buy a boat and keep it here in the winter and in New York in the summer."

"I love boats," she said. "My father has a 36-foot sailboat. I go out with him once in a while. He used to have a ski boat, too, but sold it. Things must be good in the investment banking business for you to buy this condo and a boat."

"Great. So, what do you do? Do you work, or what?"

"I do some work for my father. He owns some properties, and I help in his office. He owns that condo I'm staying in. I could never afford it on my own. What kind of boat you going to get?"

"I want a Cigarette boat."

"Well, nothing like going for speed. How big?"

"I think I'll get a 38-footer."

"That'll take you anywhere you want to go. What you gonna do, run drugs from the Bahamas?" she said laughing. "Maybe, if it pays. Nah, I'm just going to have fun with it. A boat like that is freedom, it's power, it's excellence."

"It's expensive."

"That, too, but I can afford it. I'll take you out on it, if you'd like to go."

"I'd love to. Just let me know when you get it. I'm good on boats."

That night, Hugh turned on the TV and sat in a big soft chair and stared at the TV and drank. He thought about Anne. After an hour and a half and three drinks, he took a sheet out of the linen closet, lay down on the mattress in his underwear, spread the sheet over him and went to sleep, miserable.

The next morning, Anne took the girls to their schools. Then she went to see Hugh's older brother, Dave. Dave was a counselor in the Charlotte mental health system. Where the Packard family background had given Hugh a powerful drive to gain wealth, that same background had given Dave a drive to shepherd people, like a catcher in the rye. Anne drove to his office at the Charlotte-Mecklenburg Mental

Health Center and waited until she could see him.

Dave walked around from behind his desk to greet her. He was a youthful-looking man of 39 with a few streaks of grey beginning to show in his dark hair. He was of medium build with a little paunch pushing at his waistline. He was wearing a sweater and tie.

"Come in, Anne," he said, shaking her hand. "Sit down." He walked over and closed the door. Dave's office was small and cramped, with wood-grain plywood paneling on the walls. The room was cluttered with books and papers.

"Have you heard from Hugh?"

"You know, then."

"Mother called and told me he had left without a trace."

"He called last night."

"Did he say where he was?"

"Only in Florida."

"Florida?"

"Yes. He wouldn't say where. He said he just needed some time to think things through."

"I'm so sorry."

Anne began to cry. After a moment, she spoke again.

"He just left one morning without telling me. I thought he was going to work, but he had quit his job the day before. I didn't even know. He didn't come home that night, so I called his secretary thinking he was caught at the office or something. She told me he had resigned. Imagine learning from a secretary that your husband has quit his job!"

"I bet you've been through hell," Dave said.

"I really have. I've been so depressed. I've tried to keep up a good front for the girls, but it's been hard." Anne cried some more, and Dave brought her a box of tissues. "I don't know what's happening with Hugh," she said. "I thought everything was going all right. He didn't seem to be greatly unhappy. I knew he had pressure at work, but he always has, and he's pushed himself awfully hard. They didn't fire him. He just resigned. But he didn't even tell me!"

"That hurts," Dave said.

"Yes, it really does. I thought we had a good marriage. I don't know what happened. Why didn't he tell me? I've been trying to think what I did. I must have done something to turn him away. Or maybe it's something I didn't do. I just don't know," she said.

"Maybe it's not something you did or didn't do," Dave said. "Maybe it's something that's going on inside Hugh."

"Maybe so. Why did this have to happen? I'm so angry at him!"

"I can certainly understand that," Dave said.

"I just want to knock his teeth out!"

"I can understand that, too."

Anne dabbed at her eyes with a tissue. "But I can't. Even if I could get to him, I can't tell him how angry I am. I'm afraid I would drive him away. I don't know what to do."

"He didn't give you any clues about where he is?" Dave asked.

"No, he just said he was in Florida. He said he would be in touch."

"So, all you can do is wait," Dave said.

"Yes. That's the way it looks."

"What about the girls. How are they doing?" Dave asked.

"They're doing all right. They wonder where their father is. I've told them he's away on business. I don't know how long I can keep telling them that."

"If he stays away very long, you may have to tell them the truth," Dave said.

"I know. I'll have to think about that."

"I don't know what's going on with Hugh," Dave said, "and I guess we'll just have to wait for him to let us in on it. He and I have always had a good relationship, and I might be able to help. I want to. Let me know immediately if you hear from him again."

"Thanks, Dave. I will."

She stood up to leave. Dave stood too.

"Thank you," Anne said again, extending her hand.

"You're welcome, Anne. Hang in there," Dave said.

"All right," she said, then left.

That same morning, Hugh awoke feeling groggy and laden. He went to the kitchen and put a packet into the coffee maker. Then he took out some bread and spread peanut butter and jelly on it and sat down to eat. After breakfast he took a shower and shaved. He began to feel better. The coffee and shower helped revive him. He dressed, then searched the internet for the names of several boat dealers. He wanted to look at boats, big ones. Just thinking about boats made him excited and high. Hugh had loved boats all his life, but had never been able to afford anything larger than small outboards. A boat represented freedom, and freedom was what he most wanted now. He had seen an ad for a boat that he really liked, a Cigarette boat. So he went to the Cigarette dealer first.

The dealer showed him a 39-foot Top Gun Unlimited. It was sleek and long and luxurious and fast. It had twin 700 horsepower supercharged Mercury racing engines and had been equipped with a dashboard of electronic instruments. The cabin was luxurious, plush, and comfortable. The dealer told Hugh that it came with all the required safety equipment including life jackets, and that they would give him on-the-water instruction in its operation. Hugh loved it and didn't want to look any further. The boat was outrageously expensive, as much as his new condominium, but Hugh wanted it. He asked for a price that would include the installation of stainless steel props and radar. Hugh mentally subtracted ten percent from the dealer's price and made him an offer. The dealer accepted. Then Hugh picked out some fenders and dock lines and a boat hook and other items he would need. A date was agreed upon for payment and delivery. Hugh left the dealer excited.

Driving back to the condominium, Hugh stopped at a traffic light. In the service station lot beside him was a red 1961 Corvette. It had a for sale sign on it. Hugh wanted to look at it. For years, he had wanted a Corvette like that, and he would need an extra car to keep in Florida. He went through the light, turned around and came back to the station. The car was gorgeous. It had been restored inside and out and looked like new. Within the hour, Hugh had arranged to buy it and had made a down payment. He was thrilled. He drove the Corvette back to his condominium while the service station owner drove his Porsche, and Hugh drove him back in the Corvette. Then Hugh drove his new toy out of town and onto a smooth, two-lane highway where he could try its speed and handling. He loved the guttural roar of the big American V-8 engine.

Back at his condominium, Hugh felt great. That fearful sense that the bottom would drop out and engulf him in black depression had left him. He called Margo at her office. "Hugh, are you all right?" she asked.

"I'm great!"

"You said you'd call."

"So, I'm calling," he said.

"I was worried about you. I didn't understand what was going on with you. It's good to hear your voice."

"Listen," he said. "I'm in Fort Lauderdale. I've bought a great condo."

"Fort Lauderdale! That's a long way from here."

"I love this place. Listen, the weather's perfect, I've got this great condo, I've just bought a boat, I want you to come down."

"I don't know, Hugh, it's a long way and it would take a long time to drive. I could only come on a weekend."

"You can fly. I'll buy you a ticket."

"Well, I might be able to come on a Saturday and fly back Sunday night."

"Hell, come on Friday night!"

"Maybe. I'll have to see what kind of flight I can get."

"How about this coming weekend? I miss you, Margo. I want you. We can go out on the boat. We can go to the beach. We can make love."

"I'll see. Let me check on the flights," she said. "Are you doing okay, really?"

"Yes, really. I'm doing terrific."

"Have you thought about what you're going to do?"

"I know what I'm going to do. I'm going to do what I'm doing right now," he said.

"I don't think you can do this forever," she said.

"I know. I'll worry about that soon enough. It's just great to be free!"

"Well, listen, I'll call you when I find out about flights," she said. "Where can I reach you? Do you have a new phone?"

Hugh gave her the new cell phone number.

"It will be good to see you," she said.

"It will be good to see you too," he said. "I miss you."

"I miss you too."

"Try to come Friday."

"I'll try. I'll let you know," she said.

After she had hung up Hugh called his financial advisor and told him to sell another $600,000 worth of securities. He would need the money to pay for the boat and the car and to meet living expenses. The financial advisor said he would sell the securities and wire the funds as before. Hugh went out for a relaxing supper.

Margo arrived on Friday night. Hugh met her in the Corvette.

"What's this?" she asked.

"It's a '61 Corvette," he said. "How do you like it?"

"It's great. I love it. Is it yours?"

"Yep. I just bought it."

"What about the Porsche?"

"I still have it. It's at the condo," he said.

"Hugh, you're crazy."

"I'm crazy about you!" he said, nuzzling her on the neck.

She squealed and squirted back, laughing.

On the highway, they sped toward the condominium.

Once inside the door, Hugh wrapped his arms around Margo and kissed her. He began pulling the shirttail of her blouse out of her skirt. He unfastened the clasp of her bra and ran his right hand up under the front of it to caress her breast.

"Ummm, delicious," she said.

Hugh felt himself getting hard. Margo reached down and began to caress him through his pants. He inhaled deeply and kissed her, running his tongue over her lips.

He unzipped her skirt and pushed it and her half-slip down over her hips to the floor. Soon they were in bed.

Margo awoke next morning and got out of bed to see what she could find for breakfast. The smell of coffee and warmed croissants drew Hugh into the kitchen. They ate breakfast, then Hugh, seeking elation, called the boat dealer to see if his boat was ready. It wasn't. They hadn't had time to finish installing the props and radar. It would be another day or so.

"Damn," Hugh said to Margo. "The boat's not ready."

"Oh, too bad."

"I really wanted to go out in it today. I had been looking forward to doing that with you," Hugh said, facing now a day of boredom.

"Well, we'll just have to let it wait until another time," she said. "We could go to the beach!"

"Yea. Great! We could take the Corvette!"

"Want to take a lunch or eat somewhere out there?"

"Let's take a lunch and a cooler of beer."

"Okay! Oh, I just remembered, I didn't bring a bathing suit."

"We'll buy you one."

"Okay."

"There's a nice little shopping center that's not too far from here. We can go there and see if there are any women's shops."

In the Corvette, they went to a convenience store and bought some items for lunch and a Styrofoam cooler. Then they went to the shopping center and found a beachwear store. Margo tried on three bathing suits and Hugh bought all of them. He paid for them, and Margo wore one out of the store under her blouse and shorts. Hugh put the top down on the Corvette and they sped out toward a section of beach. As he raced, Margo grew tense.

"Hugh, do you have to drive so fast? You shouldn't run through lights like that."

"What? You're not supposed to stop for yellow, are you?"

"It wasn't yellow, it was red."

"Who wants to sit at traffic lights all day?"

"You make me nervous. I'd like to stay in one piece."

"Just be cool. We'll get there okay."

It was a beautiful day, and as the sun progressed toward noon, it became almost hot, though the ocean water was still too cool for swimming, this being April. Hugh and Margo lay in the warm sun for a few minutes, then Hugh had to move. He felt restless and bored.

"Let's jog down the beach," he said.

"Hugh, can't you just sit and do nothing for once?"

"No, what's that?" He wished for a phone call and a report from the options desk. He felt empty and anxious.

They ran and walked down the edge of the surf past other sun bathers, then returned. A chilling, mid-afternoon storm drove them off the beach, ending their frustrating attempt at leisure. Hugh and Margo fought their way back to the condo through the heavy traffic of exiting beach goers. They arrived frazzled, the skin on their faces feeling slightly drawn from sun and wind.

"Let's get some coke," Hugh said.

"We've got some in the fridge."

"No, I mean cocaine. I haven't had a hit in a long time."

"Oooo. That would be fun, wouldn't it? But where can we get any?" Margo said in a suddenly playful attitude.

"We'll drive to Miami. I'm sure we can buy some on the streets there."

In the Corvette, they sped southward toward the city. Margo began to have second thoughts.

"Hugh, let's not do this. You don't know Miami. It can be a rough town. I'm scared."

"Hey, relax. It's okay. I've done this dozens of times before," Hugh said, exaggerating. "Just stay calm, little girl, and everything will be all right."

This angered Margo, and she became quiet with sulkiness, but she remained anxious.

By the time they arrived in Miami, it was dark. Not knowing the city, Hugh drove around until they found a run-down neighborhood where they saw men loitering in groups on the sidewalks. Hugh stopped near a man who stood apart from the others.

"Hey, man," he said, trying to fit his language to the subculture, "you know where we can buy some coke?"

"Not me, man, I never touch the stuff."

"Hey, do we look like cops?" Hugh guessed at the reason for his reluctance. "We just want to get a couple of hits. I'll make it worth your while." Hugh extended a $20 bill toward the man.

"Well, I don't know nothin' about it," the man said, taking the bill. "But if you ask one of the dudes on that corner, they'll know."

"Thanks, man," Hugh said, easing the Corvette over toward the group of men.

"Hugh, don't stop," Margo said, grasping his arm. "They look rough. I don't like this. Let's go."

"Take it easy, girl. We'll just go slow. It'll be all right," Hugh tried to pacify her.

"You guys know where we can get some coke?" Hugh asked generally into the group as the car pulled up to them.

They felt seven or eight pairs of eyes lock onto them as they sat in the car. Margo felt self-conscious in the costly red Corvette. She wished they were somewhere else. She clutched her blouse together tightly at the neck and had the obsessive feeling she must check the door lock, although she had locked it only a few moments before when they had entered this neighborhood.

"Maybe we do. Maybe we don't. Where'd you come from?" one man said.

"Fort Lauderdale," Hugh answered, trying to keep the quiver out of his voice. "We just drove down to get a couple of hits." His right foot flexed involuntarily on the brake pedal.

The man must have thought they were all right, because he said, "Pull over there," and pointed to a spot on the side of the street out of the light.

He spoke to another man in the group who then approached them.

"You say you want some crack?"

"We'd rather have regular cocaine," Hugh answered.

"How much you want? We got one ounce, two ounce, three ounce."

"Give us two ounces," Hugh said. Then, "How much?"

The man told him a price, and Hugh gave him the money in $20 bills as the man handed over a small plastic bag of white powder.

Done, Hugh restrained his impulse to flee and eased the Corvette away from the fearsome place and nosed it hurriedly in the direction of the freeway. He felt the tightness in his throat from stress. He hoped he could find the freeway quickly so they could get out of there. He was feeling afraid and nervous, yet exhilarated.

"Whooo!" he exclaimed as they drove away. He resisted driving the Corvette too fast through the city and attracting the attention of the police. But once on the freeway, he felt the tension flush from him and he pushed the powerful car to speed.

"We made it!"

"I thought I would die!" Margo said in a relieved, excited squeal. Her laughter filled the car as she leaned back and rolled her head backward, her hair streaming downward over the bucket seat, her white teeth glowing in the light of headlights, her eyes flashing.

Hugh froze. A cold chill encased his spine. Behind him he caught a glimpse of a police light on top of a large car.

He shot a glance at his speedometer. Way over the limit. He slowed down by lifting his foot from the accelerator. He watched the patrol car and the speedometer alternately as the Corvette sank below the limit. He could see the patrol car clearly now. Its blue light caught the flashes of passing headlights. The patrolman pulled into the left lane, but stayed behind, as though stalking its prey, then, in a burst of gasoline-induced speed, he surged forward and passed them. They watched him for a minute, then began to relax again. The incident had a sobering effect. One never knew when one was buying from an undercover officer.

Back at the condo, they were tired, but after each had inhaled some of the white powder, they soared, each in his own personal space, yet encompassing the other. All tiredness left them. Worlds of personal possibilities opened up for them. They felt they could be their best selves, accomplish their greatest life goals, win against all odds. Euphoria carried them on its golden wings to the sun.

Chapter 4

The Star Flickers

Margo's face came up to Hugh's, and she kissed his lips. Then Hugh watched her walk from the ticket counter to the security check point where with every step she disappeared farther into an indifferent maze. Once she was gone, once that body scanner swallowed her and that aircraft flew her by its prescribed schedule to Charlotte, he would be alone in the crowded terminal, surrounded by thousands of people whose eyes he might catch, for a micro-second, but with whom contact was as far away as yesterday.

Hugh turned and walked along the concourse, reviewing the sight of Margo in her red executive dress disappearing through the body scanner and flickering out of his world. He picked up his pace, hoping by physical activity to drive from him the doldrums that threatened to overtake him.

A cup of coffee might help, he thought. Then he looked at the impersonal concession with its high counter and hard-faced waitresses and picked up his step once more toward the main part of the airport and the signs that would lead him back to the parking lot and his bright Corvette.

Hugh sensed he was dangerously close to slipping into depression after the high of Margo's visit and the cocaine, and he feared more than anything else loneliness and depression. Now the car seemed to him a sweet island within a wilderness, and when he reached it, he listened with satisfaction to the throaty roar of the engine that would move him, always move him, elsewhere.

But the boat and not the car ultimately distracted him from the threatened depression. The Cigarette boat dealer called soon after he arrived back at the condominium while he prepared the cup of coffee he had wanted at the airport. The boat was ready, the man said, and

Hugh went right over. At the dealer, Hugh signed the papers and with a flair wrote the huge check that made the 39-foot Cigarette Top Gun Unlimited his. The boat was already in the water. He felt the high that comes with novelty accompanied by the anxiety of having responsibility for an unfamiliar, expensive object. This feeling drove away the looming depression and left him with the confused emotions of a sea after a passing squall.

Hugh stepped onto the gunwale and then into the cockpit and stood behind the wheel. The boat seemed enormous. It stretched out before him across a fiberglass windbreak and long expanse of foredeck toward the point of the bow. For a moment he felt incredibly high, realizing that he owned this. His dreams of having such a boat were coming true this day. He thought for that moment he might actually ejaculate with pleasure.

One of the staff mechanics, a young man with sticky blond hair that protruded beneath his cap, showed Hugh how to start the engines. The twin engines burst into vigorous life and sent cooling water gushing out the stern. The noise from the engines made it difficult to talk, and the vibration from them caused hatches to rattle. The mechanic cast off the mooring lines, thrust the transmission into forward, and powered smoothly from the T-shaped dock. The engines thrilled Hugh with their powerful roar that seemed like ten Corvettes.

The mechanic took the boat slowly toward open water near the mouth of New River, then snatched it onto a fast plane with a smooth thrust of the twin throttles. He accelerated the boat, alarming Hugh with its speed as he held on for balance, his hair whipping in the wind. Hugh had handled many runabouts, but never a boat this size and speed, and he felt uncertain about his ability. The boat was fast--faster than he had imagined, but it rode smoothly over the heavy chop of wakes from commercial and pleasure boats. He watched the mechanic carefully.

Back at the dealership, the mechanic stepped onto the dock and left Hugh in charge of his new possession. He headed for the slip at his condo. He wished he had another person on board to help with the docking, but he would just bumble through. Everything went well until he came to the dock. The boat didn't want to do what he wanted it to do. The current carried the stern sideways. A man on the shore saw the struggle he was having and took the bow line. Hugh wrestled the big, unfamiliar boat awkwardly into the slip, scraping the port side against a concrete piling. Then he stepped off the boat with a sigh of relief and congratulated himself. What a beauty! he thought.

He saw Brenda Jacobs as she walked toward her condominium.

"Hey," he called, almost ecstatic, "Come see my boat!"

Brenda walked to the dock.

"Is this yours?" she asked.

"I just got it today."

"It sure is big."

"Come on, I'll take you out on it."

"Okay, but give me a few minutes to change my clothes."

The few minutes stretched into almost 45 as Hugh waited impatiently, passing the time by reading the boat's instruction book, then the warranty. The sun on the docks was hot and bright on a day that was a forerunner of real Florida summer. Hugh scanned the skies for afternoon thunderclouds, but saw none. He became hungry and went to the marina restaurant to order some sandwiches and drinks to take with them.

Brenda finally came out wearing a stunning bandeau top and shorts. Her skin showed the smooth brown of tanning in the sun. She boarded the boat, and Hugh cranked up the engines and cast off the stern line while Brenda released the bow line. He did better getting the boat out of its slip than he had done putting it in, and they were soon gliding down a canal heading for the Intracoastal Waterway. A large marina lay on the left of the canal with huge power boats tied to piers. Ahead of them, the shores on the other side of the waterway were dotted with splendid, palm-shaded houses, many of which sported a gleaming yacht docked by a low sea wall. The sun was high in the mid-day sky, the weather was clear, and the air blowing over Hugh and Brenda felt warm on their skins. Brenda unzipped her shorts and pushed them down over her legs, revealing a tiny V of a bikini that caused a surge of desire to shoot through Hugh's groin.

He turned north on the Intracoastal Waterway, wanting to avoid the crowded area around the Port Everglades inlet. He wanted to find a stretch of calm, open water on which to accelerate the boat and get used to handling it, but much of the waterway was crowded with pleasure craft that fed into the channel from the numerous canals that joined it. While Hugh steered, Brenda set out the sandwiches and drinks that Hugh had bought, and they ate.

The going was slow with only a few stretches where the big boat could be put on a plane. With mounting frustration Hugh slowed for the frequent "Idle Speed, No Wake" zones. He reveled in the power and big feel of the boat in the short runs when he accelerated onto a plane up the channel, but he didn't think the boat was getting a proper test.

"Care for a smoke?" Brenda asked after they had passed under a low bridge at Hillsboro. She handed him a cigarette she had lit. It was marijuana.

Hugh looked at it for a second, slightly shocked, then took a full drag from it which he held in his lungs a long moment before exhaling. They shared the cigarette, and when it was a mere nub, Brenda tossed the butt over the side of the boat. As the drug took effect, things became beautiful in Hugh's eyes, even things that would not otherwise be beautiful, and things that were naturally beautiful became exquisitely so. Hugh's mood went higher than high, and he was enfolded in a sense of well-being and pleasure.

Brenda's hand touched the inside of Hugh's thigh. He looked at her. Her eyes were dreamy with the drug and she was pressing her arm against his. Hugh began looking for a place to anchor the boat. He remembered passing a small open area on the right and turned the boat around to return to Lettuce Lake. Hugh eased the boat into it and went forward to lower the anchor, securing it to the bow cleat.

Brenda went below. When Hugh came down, she was lying on the wide bed holding another marijuana cigarette. The boat rocked in the wakes of passing craft as they lost themselves in the intense pleasure of slow intercourse.

An hour later, Hugh emerged into the bright cockpit to survey where they were. The boat lay at a different angle to the shore because of a change in current, and more of the bank showed because the tide had receded slightly. He thought about Margo and felt afraid. Only that morning she had left. How could he so quickly have made love to Brenda? He dismissed what he had done as an impulse and decided not to let it happen again.

The time had come to go back to Fort Lauderdale, but Hugh was tired of the crowded waterway with its frequent drawbridges and "Idle Speed, No Wake" zones, and he wanted to take the boat offshore where it could really show its capabilities.

"I want to go back offshore," he said to Brenda when she came into the cockpit.

"Where are you going outside?" she asked.

"I saw Hillsboro Inlet on the chart just north of us. We can run out into the Atlantic there and go south to the big inlet at Port Everglades."

"Suits me," Brenda said.

Hugh nosed the racer back into the waterway and cruised slowly northward, negotiating the bridges, until they came to Hillsboro Inlet. Feeling unsure of how to run the inlet, Hugh fell in behind another boat at the last drawbridge to head for the open sea. They passed the picturesque Hillsboro Lighthouse, a metal frame structure thrusting above the palms on the northern side of the inlet. Then as they rounded the sea buoy and headed south toward Port Everglades, Hugh powered the boat onto a full cruising plane.

The Atlantic was calm with only three-foot waves and a five-to-ten knot breeze. The boat was in its element, now, and Hugh adjusted the throttles and the trim tabs, learning how to control his prize. Operating the unfamiliar craft offshore gave Hugh an anxious knot in his stomach. He ran the boat a few hundred yards offshore near the beaches still sprinkled with sun bathers in the late afternoon sun.

His idea was to run near the beach, then swing out into the Atlantic to the Port Everglades Inlet sea buoy, but he watched two small boats ahead of him stay close to the beach and head directly for the mouth of the inlet rather than swinging out to the sea buoy. He decided to follow them in. They weaved left and right, staying in a channel familiar to them. Then the two small boats took different paths. Hugh hesitated, not knowing which one to follow. He looked over the side for signs of shoals, but he saw nothing but dark green water. The sun was too low to enable him to see the sandy shoals. Hugh decided to follow the boat that in his judgment was heading toward deeper water, and swung left only to feel a bump as one of his stern drives hit bottom. He slowed the big boat, peering ahead to try to catch a glimpse of shoals. His depth sounder read only three feet. The wakes of the boats ahead of him drifted and disappeared so he could no longer follow them.

Hugh turned the boat right, believing this would take him away from the shoal he had hit. A few dozen yards of smooth running at slow speed gave him confidence that he was on the right track, then he thought he saw a shallow area ahead and cut left. He knew from the chart that a submerged breakwater lay in this area and also a shoal and a large spoil area that would be shallow. These were supposed to be marked, but he had difficulty first finding and then understanding the markers.

He decided to turn back parallel to the beach and find deeper water in which to run to the Port Everglades Inlet sea buoy. But, just as he swung the bow around toward the path over which he had come, the stern drives and hull of the racer ground into the sandy bottom, and the boat slowed to a stop. Hugh put the engines in neutral and peered over the side. The rough sand and shell bottom was visible only 18 inches below the surface. A cloud of stirred up sand swirled around the stern drives.

"We've hit bottom," he told Brenda who already was keenly aware of that fact. "I'll see if we can back off."

An outgoing current swung the stern of the boat toward the shoal. Hugh put the engines in reverse and tried to power backward against the current, but the waves lifted and dropped the propellers against the sand rendering them ineffective as the boat merely inched along the shoal and stirred up clouds of sandy murk. By now the stern had swung around so far that the boat was broadside to the swell which rolled the boat roughly from side to side. Brenda sat in a padded seat and silently held on.

Hugh shifted into neutral again and went forward along the rolling foredeck. Peering over the side in the evening light, he could see the sand all along the side of the boat only one foot beneath the surface at most. The outgoing tidal current swirled around both ends of the boat.

"Tide's pushing us farther onto the bar," he called to Brenda.

"Can't you get us off?"

"I don't know."

The three-foot waves that had seemed docile before now frightened Hugh as they rolled and lifted and dropped the boat, throwing him and Brenda about and driving the propellers against the bottom. Hugh crawled along the foredeck and back into the cockpit, then he applied reverse power again, hoping to draw the boat off backward. The boat inched over the bottom, but he could never reach water deep enough to free the propellers from the sand. The "engine hot" warning light came on for the starboard engine. Hugh ignored it and kept gunning the engines. Then the starboard engine stopped.

"Damn! I bet that engine is clogged with sand," he said to Brenda.

On the beach only a few hundred yards off, couples picked up their belongings and prepared to go in for the evening. Others strolled along the shore, holding hands, enjoying the beauty of the ocean and the sleek Cigarette boat just offshore. They did not realize the predicament Hugh and Brenda were in.

Hugh tried with the one engine to swing the stern toward deep water, but the current again overcame it. In desperation he gunned the engine, stirring up huge swirls of gushing sand with the propeller which ground against the bottom with the rising and falling waves. Then the port "engine hot" light came on. Hugh had to decide: keep trying and risk the engine, or cut the engine and save it. He cut the engine and raised the stern drives to protect the propellers. With the stern drives up, the current inexorably moved the big, proud boat farther and farther onto the shoal. Hugh climbed over the stern with an anchor and walked and swam it out against the current, hoping to keep the boat from being pushed farther onto the shoal.

"We can either stay until high tide, or we can call for help," Hugh told Brenda as he stood dripping in the cockpit.

"How long till high tide?"

"It's falling now. It could take six or eight hours. Maybe as much as ten or eleven."

"It's getting dark, Hugh. I don't think I want to stay out here all night. I'm feeling a little sick."

Hugh was feeling a little sick, too, but he didn't admit it.

"I think I could swim to shore," Brenda said.

"No way. You shouldn't try that. You should always stay with the boat. Didn't your father teach you that?"

"I know, but it doesn't look that far."

"You don't know what these currents might do."

"Okay, you're right. I'll stay here."

Hugh picked up the microphone of the VHF radio. He was not familiar with its operation, but a sticker near the radio gave an outline of instructions.

"Coast Guard, Coast Guard, Coast Guard," he called on Channel 16, "We are aground and need assistance. Repeat, we are aground and need assistance." Hugh waited for a reply which came immediately.

"This is the Coast Guard calling the vessel in need of assistance. What is your location and the identity of your vessel? Over."

"We're just north of the Port Everglades Inlet a few hundred yards from the shore," Hugh replied. "We are a 39-foot Cigarette boat, white."

"Roger, Cigarette boat, is there any immediate danger to life or property? Over."

"I don't think we're in any danger," Hugh replied. "We're just stuck on a shoal and can't get off."

"Cigarette boat, this is the Coast Guard. Please switch to Channel 22. That's Channel two two. Over."

Hugh fumbled with the digital radio until he managed to find Channel 22.

"Cigarette boat, this is the Coast Guard. Over."

"Yes. Go ahead," Hugh replied.

"Cigarette boat, how many people are on board? Over."

"Two. Myself and one crew member."

"Uh, you say you're on a shoal and not on the submerged breakwater there? Over."

"I think it's a shoal," Hugh said. "The bottom is sandy under the boat."

"Okay, Cigarette boat. Since there is no immediate danger to life or property, we cannot come get you. We could call a commercial tow company for you, but no tow boat is going to be able to help you in that area with the tide as low as it is. I suggest you wait for high tide. We'll check on you then. Over."

"Ask them when high tide is," Brenda urged.

"When is high tide?" Hugh asked.

"It will be about 0500," the voice said.

"I guess we'll just have to wait," Hugh said.

"You should wear PFDs and stand by on Channel 16. Be sure to show a light."

"Will do," Hugh said.

"Good luck," the voice said and signed off.

Hugh switched the radio back to Channel 16 and left it on. Then he turned on the stern light and pulled out two life preservers.

"We might as well settle down for the night as best we can," he said.

Brenda moodily took the bulky life preserver and put it on over her bikini, shorts and blouse. The sky was growing black over the ocean as the last light from the day faded into darkness. She went into the boat's cabin and steadied herself for a moment by gripping the edge of the galley counter. Waves pounded the side of the boat, jolting it unpredictably. The movement of the cabinet in front of her looked out of sync. Then she retched and threw up into the sink, releasing the stomach's foul smell into her nostrils. Retching again, she burst into the cockpit and threw up over the side of the boat. She remained there for a moment, hanging onto the gunwale, then turned and settled into a corner of the aft seat with her eyes closed. There she remained for a long time, silent.

Hugh started to go below into the cabin, but the smell assailed his nostrils and he quickly retreated to the driver's padded seat where he sat and braced himself against the jolting motion of the boat by pressing his feet against the starboard gunwale. Spray from waves that slopped against the seaward side of the boat wet and chilled them, but they became fixed, as though they were solidifying themselves into inanimateness to shield themselves from the ill feeling of body and soul. Hugh felt dizzy and disoriented and unable to decide even whether it was better to stay in the wet cockpit or to hazard it below. He stayed put like a reptile in stiff, reclusive hibernation.

The night for them was one of misery and helpless resignation. Exhausted, they dozed in a wakeful sleep that half shut out the elements of their plight.

Brenda was awakened by the light first.

"Hugh, wake up! There's a boat out there."

Hugh opened his eyes and turned toward the blinding searchlight that was fixed on them. Hugh stood up. The Cigarette boat rolled freely now, no longer grinding on the bottom. The land was on the other side from where it had been when they went to sleep. Waves gently lifted and dropped the boat as it strained at its anchor line off the stern. The tide had risen and freed them from the shoal.

"Ahoy, Cigarette boat, this is the Coast Guard. Are you all right?" came a voice over a loud hailer.

Hugh cupped his hands and yelled to cover the 75 yards. "I think we're okay. Can you give us a tow?"

"If you are free from the bottom, you can probably make it on your own now. You can follow us in."

"We're off the bottom," Hugh yelled, "but I'm not sure my engines will run."

"We'll stand by while you try them."

Hugh cranked the one engine he thought would be all right. It started on the second try. He started the second engine and watched for the red light. Nothing.

"I think we're okay. We'll follow you," Hugh called. Then he went to the stern to the anchor rode and tried to pull it in, but he didn't have the strength to draw the big boat to it against the waves, so he handed the rode to Brenda to pay out as they abandoned the anchor.

"All right, go ahead," Hugh called out, motioning with his arm in a waving motion toward Port Everglades.

The 22-foot rigid-hull inflatable Coast Guard boat slowly turned and headed for the inlet, feeling for the channel. Hugh looked at his watch. It was 5:25 a.m. The sky was beginning to reveal the slightest sign of lightening, showing the loom of the coming sun.

Hugh and Brenda followed the Coast Guard boat into the inlet, then the Coast Guard boat doubled back and two Coast Guardsmen deployed fenders and tied bow and stern lines to the Cigarette boat as they rafted up to make their report. Two Coast Guardsmen came aboard the Cigarette boat while a third stayed on the 22-footer.

While one guardsman asked Hugh and Brenda questions in the cockpit, the other went below.

The questions flowed mechanically. "What is your name? Where are you from? Do you have the ship's papers? What inlet did you come out? Where were you going?"

"Lieutenant?" the officer who went below interrupted them.

"Yes?"

"Look at this."

Hugh's heart sank when he saw the officer hold out the stub of a marijuana cigarette to the lieutenant.

"Where did you find this?" he said, sniffing it.

"On the floor against the berth on the starboard side. It looked like ashes scattered around on the floor, too."

"Search the boat," he said.

Brenda looked at Hugh and Hugh at Brenda. Hugh shook his head in dread.

The lieutenant went back aboard the Coast Guard boat and spoke to someone on the radio. Hugh and Brenda could see him in the dim light from the console. The sun had broken the horizon now, and the sky had burst into light. The black dome of the heavens was beginning to take on a clear, blue pallor to the east as the sun raised the curtain on a new day. A few clouds hung over the horizon, golden yellow against the silvery blue. The shore was clearly visible now.

The lieutenant returned.

"Find anything?" he asked the guardsman.

"This bag of marijuana."

Hugh held his breath. One marijuana butt and a small bag. What would it mean?

"In accordance with our zero tolerance policy, we'll have to impound your boat," the lieutenant said.

"For that little bit of grass?" Hugh burst out incredulously.

"That's the law. Marijuana is illegal, you know. You could be charged by the police, too. I'll ask you two to come aboard our boat."

Hugh looked at the three men who were ranged around them, eyes fixed on them for their response.

A look of anger flashed across Hugh's face. He shook his head as though not believing this was happening.

"All right, we'll come," Hugh said with resignation.

The lieutenant helped Brenda over the gunwale into the other boat. He grabbed Hugh by the arm to help him, too, but Hugh pulled his arm free. A guardsman took the helm of Hugh's boat.

The ride to the Port Everglades Coast Guard station was short but dreadful. Hugh sat on a fiberglass seat, head down, staring at the cockpit sole. He saw no movement before his eyes except the heels of the helmsman and that created by his own body as it swayed with the waves.

County police met the boat at the dock. With wearing thoroughness they charged Hugh with simple possession of marijuana. Hugh felt numb and didn't care anymore as he filled out a report. The police drove them back to their condominium complex.

Hugh walked silently, head lowered, exhausted, toward his door as Brenda walked toward hers. He could barely hear her speaking angrily under her breath over and over, "Son of a bitch! Son of a bitch! Son of a bitch!" Her door slammed.

Chapter 5

Flameout

A 39-foot Cigarette boat was impounded yesterday under the Coast Guard's stiff zero tolerance policy, and the Broward County Police charged the owner with simple possession of marijuana.

Hugh Packard, the boat's owner, was charged after guardsmen found the remains of one marijuana cigarette on the boat. Brenda Jacobs, a crew member on board at the time, was not charged. The Coast Guard had boarded the craft in Port Everglades to fill out a routine report after Packard had called for help when the boat went aground just offshore north of the Port Everglades Inlet.

This is the seventh yacht seized this year under the Coast Guard's zero tolerance policy, and a Coast Guard spokesman...

The story made *The Miami Herald.* A picture of Hugh's Cigarette boat impounded at the Coast Guard station appeared beside the article.

Damn, Hugh thought when he saw the article. It's not bad enough to have your brand new boat confiscated, it's got to be spread all over the newspapers for your humiliation. He was just glad he didn't know many people in the Miami area.

Hugh saw Brenda only once after that. The day after the boat fiasco he saw her walk to her car with a suitcase. She didn't come back and never communicated with him again. He assumed she was living in another of her father's real estate acquisitions.

Hugh drank more. He didn't go out much. Only once did he go to the Coast Guard station to see his impounded boat, two days after the incident. He hired a lawyer in Miami.

The eyes of a sharp business editor at *The Charlotte Observer* caught the name of Hugh Packard in *The Miami Herald*, a sister newspaper. The name rang a bell for him because he had written an article months before about a stellar Fortress Securities derivatives trader by the same name. Given the flamboyant specter of the Cigarette boat in the picture, he thought it might be the same person.

The editor called Fortress and learned that Hugh had resigned. When he asked for his whereabouts, he was told he had moved to Florida.

A call to an editor at *The Miami Herald* sent a reporter to check the Coast Guard and police reports.

Hugh's cell phone rang.

"I'm trying to reach Hugh Packard, the securities trader," the voice said.

"This is he," Hugh replied.

"This is Harry Worth at *The Charlotte Observer*. I did an interview with you when you were at Fortress Securities."

"Yes, I remember you," Hugh said, confirming for Harry the fact that he was the same Hugh Packard. "What can I do for you?"

"I saw in *The Miami Herald* that you had had your boat confiscated on a marijuana charge," he said.

Go to hell, Hugh wanted to say and hang up the phone. But he caught himself.

"Yes. A passenger on my boat brought one marijuana cigarette," he fudged. "I didn't even know she was bringing it on board. But I was the skipper and I got charged and they took my boat. That's life, I guess, but I'll get the boat back, and they can't make the marijuana charge stick."

"That's too bad." The editor sounded skeptical. "So, what are you doing in Fort Lauderdale?"

"I'm starting a new base of operations," Hugh said, seizing the moment. "I'll be going with a New York securities firm and specializing in options in mergers and acquisitions. I'll be establishing a power team with the best traders in the business and the most sophisticated computerized trading equipment."

"Sounds interesting," the editor said. "I'll be watching for your name in *The Wall Street Journal*."

The Miami Herald story ran in *The Charlotte Observer*, complete with a copy of the photograph of Hugh's boat and his and Brenda's names. Nothing was mentioned about Hugh's career plans.

Alone at breakfast, Margo felt a jolt when she saw the story in the paper.

I know Hugh is upset about this, she thought. I wonder why he didn't tell me when we talked on the phone last night.

Then a possible reason filtered into her brain as she connected the name "Brenda Jacobs" with Hugh's silence, and she felt anger shoot through her. It was a connection she didn't want to make.

He probably just had her out for the afternoon, she thought, wanting not to believe.

The advent of Brenda bothered her, and she found she couldn't concentrate on her work all morning wondering about this phantom who had entered the scene. Margo was planning to fly back to Fort Lauderdale in ten days, and she wanted to know more.

Maybe I should wait and talk with Hugh about this when I get down there, but I want to talk to him now, she debated with herself. I could call him and find out how he's doing under the pressure of being charged and having his boat confiscated. At least then he would know I know.

"Hugh, I saw in the paper where your boat was confiscated by the Coast Guard," she told him on the phone. "Are you all right?"

"I was afraid that would make the papers up there," Hugh said. "It's no big deal. They found one marijuana cigarette and took my boat. But I'll get it back. I've got a law firm working on it."

"I'm sorry. I know that was a blow to have your new boat taken and to be charged. How are you doing?" Margo sounded sympathetic.

"I'm okay. No problem. I try to stay busy. How about coming down this weekend?"

"Hugh, I'm planning to come weekend after next, you know."

"You could come both. I'm paying for the tickets."

"I just can't. I have things I've gotta do here. But I'll see you weekend after next. That won't be so long."

"I really miss you and wish you were here. It's boring without you."

Margo wanted to ask if Brenda Jacobs helped him fill his empty hours, but she decided not to risk the question.

After hanging up she thought, I'm not sure I can put up with this. If Hugh is seeing another woman, it will tear me apart. I've had enough of that in one life. I don't want to lose him, but there are worse things. I like Hugh, I think I love him. We'd make a good team. We could be prosperous together. But only if our relationship can be happy.

She thought about her past experiences with the torments of unfaithful men and reaffirmed to herself that she would not tolerate such pain again.

Anne saw the newspaper article, too, that same day, only later, after she had gotten the girls off, and only after her friend Sally had called her to tell her it was there.

"Look at this," Ken had said to Sally at the breakfast table. "Hugh Packard has been charged with possession of marijuana and has had his boat impounded."

"What?" Sally said. "Let me see that."

Sally stood behind Ken's chair and they read the article simultaneously.

"That looks bad," Sally said. "And he had a woman with him. This is really going to hurt Anne. I hope she doesn't see it."

"She's going to see it," Ken said. "It's right here in the paper."

"But maybe she'll miss it."

"It's not going to do her any good to miss it because other people will see it, and eventually she'll find out. It's better for her to know."

"I guess you're right," Sally said. And because she decided Ken was right, she called Anne, to be her friend, to be with her if she had seen the article and to break it to her gently if she hadn't.

"Anne, have you seen the article in the paper?" Sally asked on the phone.

"No. What article?"

"There's an article about Hugh in the paper this morning. You better read it. It says he was charged for possession of marijuana and they confiscated his boat. You read it and I'll come over and we can talk."

Sally didn't mention Brenda Jacobs. She knew Anne would see her name.

At Anne's breakfast table, Sally watched Anne pore over the article for a second time. Her face was taut. The muscles in her neck were hard, and Sally could see her pulse throb in her throat.

"I wonder what's going on with Hugh." Anne said, mystified. "I didn't even know he had a boat. Could there be a mistake? Could this be another Hugh Packard?"

"I don't know," Sally said. "The newspaper says it's Hugh Packard, the Charlotte securities trader. It must be him."

"I can't believe this. I've wondered if Hugh ever smoked marijuana. I knew some of his friends did. He could be getting into real trouble."

"It doesn't look good, does it?"

"There was a woman with him. Did you see that?" Anne asked, as though maybe that fact didn't really exist.

"Yes, I saw."

Anne sat silent for a moment, staring at the newspaper. Her cheeks sagged in depression. Her forehead wrinkled like a baby about to bawl. Her head shook slightly from side to side, trying not to believe, but believing.

"Damn it! I hate him! I hate him! I hate him!" Anne was standing, pounding her fist into the article against the table, dissolving into fiery tears. Sally sat riveted to her chair, galvanized by the sudden explosion in her friend. She stood up and took her friend from behind by the shoulders. Anne shook and wept, then put her hand on her friend's hand. After a minute, she sat straight down in the kitchen chair under her, still crying.

Sally stayed with her that day. Ken took care of their children. Anne cried and slept and didn't eat. Sally picked up Anne's children and told them mommy was sick.

Rain swept in sheets across the runway as Margo's plane touched down and taxied to the terminal. She looked out the window of the plane, wondering what she would find when she found Hugh.

"Hi, Sweets," he said as she re-entered his life by walking out of the gate area, adding warmth to the cold terminal.

"Hello, Hugh," she tried to make the words express a warmth she had once felt. He kissed her and took her bag, and they walked side by side through the crowded baggage area.

The rain was blowing sideways across the parking lot and wet Margo's stockings and Hugh's pants as they walked to the Porsche.

"Where's the Corvette?" Margo asked.

"I left it at the condo. It leaks around the canvas top," Hugh said.

They drove through the rain toward Hugh's condominium, and the rain compressed them within the confines of the car, pressing upon them the question that hung in the air. Margo wanted to ask it, but not now, not so soon after getting back together. Later would be better, after they had settled in with each other again and felt secure.

They made small talk in the car, and at the condominium Margo dashed for the door holding her jacket over her head against the rain. Inside, she shook the water out of her hair, and Hugh began to take the wet clothes off of her. They made love in an almost perfunctory way, without intense feeling, as though doing that would glue them together while the lingering question threatened to rend them apart.

Hugh lit a cigarette.

"I didn't know you were smoking," Margo said.

"I just started back again."

"I wish you wouldn't. It's not good for you."

"Look, don't bug me about it, okay? I won't get hooked again."

"Okay. It just smells bad, that's all."

"Let's drop the subject."

"So, how's it been going?" Margo asked.

"Great," Hugh lied.

"Any news about getting your boat back?"

"Not yet. They've still got it, but I'll get it back. They can't just take a person's property like that when it wasn't even my marijuana."

"So, whose marijuana was it?"

There it was. The question.

"It was that damned bitch's," Hugh said, trying to reject the emerging threat. "She brought the marijuana on board, and I got blamed for it."

"That was the Brenda Jacobs mentioned in the paper?"

"Yes, what a bitch. I hope I never see her again."

"Where did you meet her?"

"Oh, she had a condo a couple of doors away. I just ran into her in the parking lot."

"How many times did you see her?"

"We had a drink together. I took her out for a ride on the boat. That was it. Why all these questions? I told you she was a bitch!" Hugh was getting angry.

"If she was such a bitch, why are you getting so defensive?" Margo retorted.

"I'm not getting defensive," Hugh said. "I just want you to know there's nothing to it and I'm through with her. Can't we just drop it?"

"I need to know, Hugh. It's important to me. When I have a relationship with someone, it's important to me to be able to trust him. Please try to understand this thing from my point of view, Hugh. I don't want to be hurt. I've been hurt before. I love you and I want to know that you love me. If you love me you won't do anything to hurt me. It hurts a little that you took this woman out."

"She's nothing to me. She's just a bitch."

"But you met her and you wanted to take her out."

"She was around. She liked boats."

"You took her out the same day you dropped me off at the airport. That hurts."

"It just happened to be the day I got my boat."

"Did you smoke marijuana with her?"

Hugh didn't answer.

"Hugh, did you smoke with her on the boat?"

"Yea."

"Did you make love to her?"

"Would I make love to a bitch like that?"

"I don't know, Hugh. Maybe you didn't think she was such a bitch just then. Did you?"

"Did I what?"

"Make love to her."

"Hell, no!" Hugh said in a sharp, angry tone.

Margo contemplated his response. "I don't believe you," she said.

"Well, just what am I supposed to do if you don't believe me? Get a legal affidavit? I said I didn't make love to her. That's that."

"Your voice just doesn't ring true, Hugh. And I know you're capable of playing around."

"What are you, paranoid or something? How could you feel insecure over a little bitch like that?"

Margo looked out the sliding glass doors at the rain wetting the patio, and beyond it the sodden spring grass and the canal roughened like sandpaper by the raindrops. She wished she were back home in Charlotte.

"I'm tired of this, Hugh," she said, still staring out the doors.

"Look," Hugh implored, "I said there was nothing to her. Let's forget it."

"No, I mean I'm tired of this whole thing. I'm tired of wondering when you're going to get your life together. I'm tired of spending my weekends flying down here. I'm tired of being the 'other woman' and not knowing when there will be yet another woman."

"I'm sorry, Margo. I promise there won't be any more women."

"What about Anne?"

"Anne? What about her?"

"Have you decided what to do about Anne?"

"No, I haven't. It's not that simple. I have two daughters, you know." Hugh was getting angry again.

"Have you thought about what it does to me that you're married?"

"Look, you knew I was married when you got into this. Nothing's changed. I still love you."

"Maybe so, but I can't go on and on like this. There has to be some resolution. I have to know we have some future together."

"I still have some things to work out."

"Well, when do you think you'll get it all worked out? Next year? Five years from now?"

"I don't know."

Margo drew a deep breath and let it out. She looked away again, out the glass doors. The rain was still turning the world grey.

I'm getting out, Hugh, she thought to herself, but her lips didn't form the words.

"Have you contacted any New York investment firms, Hugh?" Margo asked at supper.

"Yea, a couple."

"What kind of response did you get?"

"They sounded very positive. They're trying to work things out."

"When will they let you know?"

"I don't know. These things take time. The process probably would have moved faster if I hadn't left Fortress already."

"I'm worried about you Hugh. I think you may be headed for a dead end."

"Nah, I'll find the right position. Besides, that's my business."

"It's my business, too, if I'm hooked up with you!"

"Listen, we don't have any commitments, right? That's our understanding, right?"

"Yes, but I can't just be neutral toward you. I love you. I care about what happens to you and to us."

"Well, I appreciate your concern, but that's something for me to work out."

"Well, I just want you to know that what you do affects me, too. When you quit your job and go hauling off to Florida spending money like there was no tomorrow, I just don't know what to expect from you."

"Look, just calm down, okay? Everything is fine."

"Just don't expect me to come flying down here every weekend. I have a career back home, you know, and I have other things to do with my weekends than fly off to be with you."

"Listen, I told you, everything is fine. I've got money. I don't need a job. I'm doing great! And if you don't want any part of it, there are plenty of other women around who do!"

"What do you mean by that?"

"Just that. Look around. There are women everywhere just waiting to jump at a chance to go with someone like me."

"Hugh, you just don't care, do you? A relationship means nothing to you. All you care about is a good screw. Well, I'll tell you this, friend, I don't need it. I don't need that. I won't be jerked around all over the country following you on some fantasy."

"Fine, so don't."

"I won't, believe me. Hugh, I don't think this is going to work for me. I mean, maybe you've got what you want right now, but it's just not for me. I like having a little order in life. I like to know what's coming. I just can't count on you. I'm pulling out."

"What do you mean by that?"

"I'm pulling out of the relationship. I've had enough."

Hugh looked stunned. He wanted to back up. He had said too much, been too careless. He felt a black chasm opening under him.

"Look, I'm sorry," he said.

"I am too, but I just have to get out."

"I'll get straightened out."

"Eventually, maybe, but I'm not going to wait."

"Margo, I need you. You're everything to me."

"If I mean so much to you, why are you still married to Anne? Why is there a Brenda Jacobs in your life?"

"I told you. I'm the father of two little girls. It's not that simple. And Brenda was absolutely nothing."

"I'm sorry, Hugh. That's not good enough. I'm getting out."

"Don't do this, Margo," Hugh commanded.

"I have to," Margo answered.

Hugh looked at the floor and shook his head. He went into the bedroom, closed the door, and lay down on the bed. Margo slept on the couch that night. Next morning, she got up early, ate breakfast, dressed and called a cab.

"Don't call a cab, Margo. I can take you to the airport," Hugh said, coming into the kitchen.

"I'd rather do it this way, Hugh. Let me go," Margo said.

The cab took her to the airport. She arrived at 8:15 a.m. Her plane wouldn't leave until 3:35 p.m. She spent a long seven hours reading magazines and walking around until her flight left.

A person walking into Hugh's condominium a month later would not have recognized it as the same place, nor Hugh as the same man.

Dirty dishes filled the sink and covered the counter top and range, dripping sauces and crumbs. Clothes hung on every conceivable hook--door knobs, chair backs, door tops, bed posts--or lay on the floor in dirty piles, or hung askew in the closet. The bedroom had a dank, locker-room smell like ripe gym shoes.

The nearly-empty refrigerator contained only bottles of ketchup, mustard, souring milk, leftover beans and skinless potatoes looking suspicious in uncovered bowls, and several cans of beer. Two forgotten bananas lay melting into soft, brown puddles on top.

Hidden in the laundry basket was a small plastic bag of marijuana. Cocaine had been there, too, but was now gone. The undisposed trash contained empty bourbon and wine bottles.

The drapes were drawn against the light of day and the prying eyes of neighbors, making the inside of the luxury condominium dark and cave-like. Neighbors, their curiosity aroused by the shut-up unit and the muffled sounds that emanated from it, discussed Hugh around umbrella-covered tables at the swimming pool. No one had seen Hugh much in recent weeks, although they thought he was at home because of the low bumps and noises they heard and the irregular lights that illuminated the curtains at night.

Finally, one matronly woman, out of curiosity and feigned concern, knocked at Hugh's door one morning.

Through the closed door, Hugh asked,

"Yes? Who is it?"

"It's Mabel Turnbul. I'm one of your neighbors."

Hugh opened the door slowly. Light fell on his unshaven face and caused his eyes to squint. He was wearing a plain tee shirt and dark trousers. He saw a stout, grey-haired woman in her 70s standing before him.

"What can I do for you?" he asked.

"I just wanted to see if you are all right, Mr. Packard. We hadn't seen you out in a while."

"Yes, I'm fine. I've had a touch of the flu or something, but I'm okay now. Thank you for stopping by, but please don't worry about me." With that, he began closing the door.

"I hope you feel better. Let me know..." but Mrs. Turnbul didn't get to finish the sentence because the door shut tightly.

After closing the door, Hugh went to the kitchen, ran some water in a pan, turned on the stove, and dumped yesterday's coffee residue out of a mug so he could refill it with today's. He found a nearly-empty box of cereal and dumped its contents, including crumb-dust, into a bowl. From a wrapper he removed a slice of bread and put it in the toaster. Then he sat and thought. This was the start of another day, a day that would hold only long hours of dull, hurting consciousness. He could think of nothing to do to fill those hours, and if he had thought of something, he would not have had the energy to do it.

A stack of *Wall Street Journals* lay beside the couch, unread. The laptop sat on a small, cluttered desk, its screen saver running. Piles of printed investment information and lists of options with their prices and dates spilled over beside the laptop. Hugh hadn't touched them in days, nor had he contacted any brokerage firms in New York recently. He was aware that he had no drive, and he despised himself for it with a cold hatred.

He felt nothing except the dull hurt. It was an inexplicable hurt, as though he had been born unknowingly with a sharp pain but had never become conscious of it because he had never known existence without it. It was a hurt of the unconscious. He did not love, not even when he thought of Anne or Margo or the children, or his mother or brother, or himself. He tried to decide if he cared if he did not love. He decided it made no difference.

When he looked out at the dock at his recovered boat, which the Coast Guard had returned to him, he felt no quickening of excitement. The lines were slack, the boat slouched crooked in its slip, and green algae had begun to grow on the sides where the bottom paint failed to reach high enough.

Once, he wished Anne would call. But, of course, he hadn't given her his new number. She had his old number, which would work. He couldn't call her because he was afraid he couldn't speak well enough to present himself as a whole person. Instead, he sat and stared and thought. He was beyond weeping, and was like those most pitiful souls in the deepest circle of Dante's hell, frozen in the ice.

He thought about suicide, objectively and without passion. Philosophically, he thought he was open to it. How would he do it? What would be his preferred method? Car accident? Drowning? Gun shot? Drug overdose? He turned each over in his mind, running through a test scenario, then he lost track of his thoughts. He found it difficult to concentrate on any subject for very long.

He became a creature of the night, staying inside during the day and going out after dark. One evening Hugh returned from the convenience store with bread and cereal and milk. He parked the Corvette and walked under the street light toward his unit. A cockroach dashed halfway across the concrete walk and stopped, probing with its antennae. Hugh almost raised his foot to crush the life out of it, then stopped and stared at it. It seemed so full of life, and its life was so simple. I envy that damned cockroach, he thought. Jolted, he went inside to call his brother Dave.

Chapter 6

Anne

"Hugh called," Dave told Anne on the phone. "He's all right. He's in Fort Lauderdale and he gave me his new cell phone number."

"Oh, I'm glad to find out where he is. Could you give me the number?"

"I'll give it to you, Anne, but I think you'd better not call him."

"Why not?"

"He's very depressed and I think he needs to be left alone until he can get hold of himself. He's got a lot of problems to deal with."

"What kind of problems?"

"Wait 'til I talk with him in person and I'll be able to tell you better. It seems very complicated."

"Is he having an affair?" Anne asked.

"Anne...he was. But I think it's over."

"Damn him!" Anne said, “I was afraid of this." She began to cry.

"Give him some time. I think he'll come out of it eventually."

"Great, and what about me? When will I come out of it?"

"I know it must hurt terribly, Anne."

"You're damned right it does!"

"I'm going down there as soon as I can work out my schedule. He's hurting and he needs to talk. I think he may be ready to make some changes."

"Well, all I can say is good luck. You let me know when you're going and how things come out, okay?"

"Yes, of course."

"I'm glad to know where he is, I think."

Dave laughed. "I know what you mean," he said.

"Keep me in touch, Dave."

"Okay, I will."

Anne felt the anger rising in her chest. Her mind raced with admonitions. She leaned against the kitchen counter and thought.

He was hurting! What about me? What about the weeks I've spent depressed and not knowing where he was or what he was doing? What about the hours I've spent worrying about the girls? He was hurting! So, damn him! If he's hurting, maybe that's the price he needs to pay for what he's done. Let him hurt, damn him! We certainly have hurt enough. What's he got to hurt about?

The sight of Hugh's credit card bills on the kitchen counter fired her anger even more.

He goes off to Florida spending all our money without even so much as letting us know where he is. The bastard!

She took a deep breath and turned her thoughts to the things she needed to get done that day. The main problem was the crack in the wall. She and Hugh had built the house and moved into it less than a year before, but she was having to iron out all the new house difficulties. After she had called the builder repeatedly to complain, a man representing him was coming out to the house that day. Then there were the usual domestic tasks involving the children and the housework.

The builder's representative arrived late in the afternoon. "Hello, ma'am, I understand you've got a crack somewhere?"

"Right out by the garage. I'll show you."

Anne took him around the outside of the house to a place where the brick carport joined the main part of the house. A crack in the wall started at the top and ran down about six feet, a quarter of an inch wide at its worst.

"Oh, that's nothing to worry about, ma'am, you get a little settling. All new houses do it."

"Just a little settling!" Anne's voice almost rose to a scream. "The wall is cracking in half! The damned garage is falling off, and you say it's just a little settling! That's not supposed to happen, and you'd better make it right!"

"Well, ma'am, I don't know what we could do now. We'll come out and fill in the crack if you'd like."

"No! I want you to fix it and make it stop cracking," she said.

"It ain't so bad. Just a little settlement crack. Tell you what. We'll fill it, and if it gets any worse, we'll take another look at it."

"It's shoddy. It looks like hell. The damned garage is falling off. What's the matter with you people! Can't you do anything right!"

Anne's anger was overflowing.

"And this isn't the first problem I've had," she said. "I had trouble with the toilet in the girls' bathroom. It made sewage run out on the floor. The damn thing overflowed! And I noticed water leaking around the base of the toilet. I couldn't get through to you people, so I had a plumber come out, and he had to take the toilet out and install a new pipe under it and fix the seal. You pay seven hundred and twenty five thousand dollars for a house and you get shit in the floor! I'm sending you the bill. And if you don't fix this crack, we're going to sue!"

"Now, lady, you didn't really have shit in the floor."

“Shit, sewage, pee, whatever you want to call it, it stank and it shouldn't have happened!"

Anne spun around and walked back into the house, leaving the man standing by the cracked wall, her usual poise vaporized in the face of the conflict. She shoved her rump against the stiff door to close it, then, resting against it, she began to cry.

Where the hell are you when I need you, Hugh, she thought. I don't know how to sue anybody. I have to fight these fights by myself. Get yourself back here! She wiped her eyes with a tissue. I want to erase these last few weeks, she thought. Pretend they never happened. It's been a bad dream. How could you do this?

The house had become a major burden to her, and Hugh was the one who had wanted it. As soon as he had made it big in investments, he had wanted this giant house in Quail Hollow. They had bought this lot and hired an architect to design a house that would make a good appearance in this posh neighborhood bordering the Quail Hollow Club.

The house was on a street lined with massive, two-story brick residences. To drive down the street was to feel overwhelmed by the towering dwellings. The feeling the houses gave a visitor was a sense of great wealth, and that inflamed Hugh's desire to live in this neighborhood of seeming financial giants.

The two-story brick houses lined both sides of the street and rose massively out of their treeless lots like Easter Island statues, stone faced and impenetrable. Most of the houses had expensive details such as fluted columns, slate roofs, fan windows, solid wrought iron railings and brick gate posts with brass lanterns. Some were on the Quail Hollow golf course.

Professional landscape crews preened the neighborhood, spraying shrubs and lawns with chemicals from new tank trucks and unloading mowing machines from trailers to cut and trim and edge the deep green grass.

The neighborhood was raw with newness, but it spoke of wealth and stature. One could imagine that in 50 years this would be another street like Charlotte's Queens Road with its soaring oak trees, old-money mansions, and wide lawns. Only things like an occasional basketball goal over a garage door broke the spell and served as a reminder to casual visitors that human beings lived in Quail Hollow.

Other, temporary evidences of a human presence abounded at the several sites where houses were still under construction. Garish yellow portable toilets stood intrusively on the edges of these yards close to the road where they made their human statement in the most public way. Clods of mud smeared the road, tracked there by construction machinery. Stacks of concrete blocks and chimney flue and piles of debris stood beside the road. Noise from cement trucks and power saws and hammers wracked the elegant peace. And mingling into the grimy construction scene were stylish young women in tennis dresses off to the club in their new, European cars.

Within this unsettled yet elegant scene Anne's emotions slammed her. The anger was easy enough for her to understand, even though it was not easy to shake off. Hugh was the culprit, and the more Anne learned about Hugh's activities, the easier it became for her to blame him for the calamity that was destroying their dream.

The guilt Anne felt was more difficult for her to understand. She was assaulted by doubts. What had she done to bring this on? How had she let Hugh down? Why did he feel it necessary to turn to another woman? Where had she failed? She could think of no answers to her questions and at the same time hundreds of answers, so many that none was satisfactory. Maybe she should have taken more interest in investments. Maybe she should have gone running with him more. Maybe she gave too much love to the girls and not enough to him. Maybe God was punishing her for the sexual experimenting she had done as a college student. Her reason told her she shouldn't feel guilty, but she judged herself nonetheless and found plenty of fault.

One afternoon Anne sat in a darkened den as the minutes passed nearer to the time to pick up the girls from their schools. She sat motionless in a chair, her legs sprawled, her arms resting on the stuffed arms, staring at the blank television screen. Time seemed suspended. She couldn't make her legs move to start her toward the car to pick up the children. Her universe was dark. Only her motherly sense of duty and the inexorable upticks of the digital clock toward the appointed time eventually stirred her to move to pick them up.

Elizabeth came out that day with a note from her teacher, who said she was concerned because Elizabeth's work wasn't up to par and she seemed unhappy. Anne read it. "So, how was school today?" Anne asked her as soon as she was strapped in her seat belt.

"It was all right."

"Just all right? Nothing special happened?"

"Nah."

"Are you feeling okay?"

"Not really. I don't feel good."

"Anything hurt?"

"No. I just don't feel good."

Anne put her hand on Elizabeth's forehead, not expecting to feel any fever. She didn't.

"You don't have a fever," she said, as though the words might dismiss the problem, but she felt their emptiness. She feared that Hugh's delinquency was troubling Elizabeth, but she didn't know how to cure that illness.

"I want Daddy to come home."

"I know. I do too." Anne said this, but she wasn't sure she meant it. Sometimes she hoped Hugh would disappear from her awareness forever.

"When's he coming home?"

"It won't be long." Anne tried to be optimistic.

"He sure has been gone a long time."

"I know, but he'll be back soon."

Angie, whom Anne had picked up earlier, had remained silent through all this, sitting in the back seat, turning the pages of a book.

"Why did Daddy go away?" Angie asked, innocently raising the unanswerable question.

And since Anne couldn't answer it, she felt angry and inadequate and continued the lie she had begun.

"You know he had business to do," she said.

"Why doesn't he call?"

"He's very busy."

"Does he still love us?"

"Sure he does. He'll be back. You'll see."

"I want him to come back now."

Anne pulled into the driveway, relieved to be able to end this conversation.

"Okay, girls, get your things. All out. Do you want to go to the Sterling's house? I'll call Sally."

Inside the house, Anne felt exhausted, even though the time was only early afternoon. She called Sally Sterling and arranged to take Elizabeth and Angie over there. She hoped she would have a chance to talk with Sally alone this afternoon.

Anne had been planning a trip to her parents' home in Richmond. It was a long 250-mile trip by car, and she had been assaulted by fears. She had never been afraid to drive long distances before, but lately whenever she thought about driving with the girls to Richmond she felt afraid, so afraid she was thinking about not going.

She imagined the worst scenarios: a car accident...her lying bleeding beside the road...the girls injured and helpless. Or, a mechanical breakdown...she and the girls having to walk miles to the nearest service station...two men in a rusty pickup truck with a shotgun in a rack stop to "offer them help," but really are rapists and molesters. Anne felt paralyzed with fear. She couldn't make up her mind to go, but she couldn't back out. She was losing confidence in herself. She wanted to talk it over with Sally.

But Marilyn Arrington was at Sally's house when Anne arrived. Marilyn had come to Sally's in her own desperation. While the children played and chattered in the den, the women talked in the kitchen.

"This custody battle is really heating up," Marilyn said, while Sally took out mugs for coffee and Anne sat at the breakfast table with her legs crossed and arms folded. Marilyn sat across from her.

"I can't understand Trot," Marilyn said. "He never seemed to care about the children when we were together. He almost never did anything with them. Now, you'd think they were his whole life. He wants joint custody, and his lawyer says if I don't give it to him he is going to try to discredit me as a parent because of the affair I had years ago."

Sally opened a drawer and took out spoons, then walked across the kitchen and removed a basket of coffee packets of different flavors from a cabinet.

"Anne, you might as well know about that," Marilyn said, not realizing that Anne had already heard about the affair from Sally. "I had an affair with a man about four years after Trot and I were married, but I broke it off and put it behind me. Now Trot is going to have his lawyer use that against me to get my children.

“He's the one who had the bad affair. It was his affair that put this marriage on the rocks. Now I have to bring up his affair in court to try counteract his charges against me. I hate this! We're killing each other. I never knew people could act this way."

Sally poured half and half into a small, glass pitcher and set it in the middle of the table.

"The lawyers do it," Marilyn said. "You hire a lawyer to defend you and they go after your mate with knives. Trot is trying to keep everything he can. He doesn't want to give me enough child support if I do get the children and doesn't want me to have the house. We built the house together. It's the only place the children have ever lived. It's in the best school district. We're accustomed to this. I don't want to move to another neighborhood, and we can't afford to buy a new house in our neighborhood. He wants to sell the house and throw us out. He doesn't give a damn if we end up in an apartment or what. He's fighting me on every front. It's got me so upset!"

Sally reached for the basket of coffee packets so they could have another cup. Then she poured water into the coffee maker.

"Why does he want the children?" Marilyn said. "What's he going to do with them? How's he going to take care of them? It's so stupid! He's only fighting because he doesn't want his self-esteem injured. He'll have to put them in day care, and he works late a lot, so he won't be able to pick them up. He'll have to hire someone else to do that, unless he marries again. I don't want Wayne and Sharon to live in that situation with a stepmother. The whole damn thing makes me sick!"

Sally and Anne listened without commenting, stunned by the violence of it all.

"What kind of settlement do you want, Marilyn?" Sally asked.

"I'm willing to give him visitation rights, but I think the children should live with me. He could have them every other weekend and for two weeks in the summer, and he could pay medical expenses and extra school expenses and things that come up. He should give me child support, and I should have the house. He can afford it, believe me. He makes plenty of money."

"That sounds like a typical sort of settlement," Sally said.

"What makes it so bad is he won't talk to me," Marilyn said. "He hasn't spoken to me in weeks. I don't know what he's plotting. His lawyer calls me. It scares me. And I have to fight. Sometimes I just want to give up and not ask for anything, but if I do I'll be in poverty the rest of my life. I know too many women who have gotten raw deals in divorce cases. They end up with nothing. It's just not fair."

Anne put artificial sweetener and half and half in her coffee and stirred. Sally sat down with them at the table.

"Then I get these scary phone calls at night," Marilyn said. "The phone rings and I answer it, and there's no sound. Sometimes it happens in the middle of the night. I think it's Trot, but I can't be sure. I hang up, and in a few minutes the phone rings again and it's the same thing. Then I'm all awake for a couple of hours. It's unnerving. I think Trot is waging a psychological war. He hates me. He's trying to wear me down. He thinks I'll get tired of all this and just give up and let him have whatever settlement he wants. Well, I'm not giving up. I'm fighting for my children and I'll fight till I drop. Wouldn't you?" she nodded toward Anne.

"Yes...I guess I would." Anne just wanted somehow to wave a magic wand or pray and create peace. That was her nature. She thought she could never fight a court battle such as the one Marilyn was going through.

As much as Anne wanted to talk about Hugh, she had held back, listening to Marilyn's story. But, because she was hurting so much, she ventured a bit of her pain.

"Hugh has gone off to Florida," she said softly. "And I just found out he's definitely had an affair."

"I thought so," Sally said.

"Welcome to the real world," Marilyn said.

"He called his brother Dave and told him he's in Fort Lauderdale. Dave found out he's definitely had an affair, but he says he thinks it's over and he's ready for some changes. Dave is going down there to talk with him. I can't even call him yet."

"Well, we thought he might have had an affair when we saw that woman's name in the paper," Sally said, recalling the conversation she had had with her friend.

"I saw that article," Marilyn said. "It sounded like he was having a pretty wild time.

Better get yourself a lawyer, Anne. He can walk all over you if you don't."

"But I don't want a lawyer," Anne said. "I don't want to go through a fight like you're going through."

"Hey, I didn't want it either, but I've learned a few things the hard way, and I've talked with some other women who are going through divorces. You'd be amazed how they've been dumped on because they wanted to keep things peaceful and friendly. You'd better get the best lawyer you can find and do what he says. That's what I'd advise you to do." Marilyn finished stirring her coffee and put her spoon on the table with a clank.

"You have to do what you think is right for you, Anne," Sally said. "You haven't even talked with Hugh, and you don't want to do anything too quickly. You don't want to get run over, but you don't really know if that will happen yet. I don't think it would hurt to wait and see."

"Yes, I think I'll wait. I don't want a divorce. I'm very angry at Hugh. I think what he has done is terrible. I don't know if I can love him after this. I'm really confused and I don't know what I'll do. I have to talk to Hugh."

"How are the girls taking it?" Sally asked.

"Fairly well, but I can tell it's having an effect. Elizabeth is not doing well in school. She looks worried."

"Have you talked with your parents about it?" Sally asked.

"Yes, and they're mad as hell," Anne said. "They think Hugh's lost his mind. They're ready for me to come home and live with them. I was planning to drive up to see them, but...and this is hard to understand...I've been so afraid to drive. I don't know why, but when I think about taking the girls by myself that far, I just imagine all kinds of awful things happening. This has never happened to me. I've driven to Richmond before, even with the girls. But I just have this awful feeling that we'll be killed or raped..."

Anne began to cry. Sally stood up to get her a tissue.

"It's pretty scary. I know what you mean," Marilyn said. "I've been so afraid that I couldn't make it financially without Trot. I mean, this is an expensive world we live in. And you hope you can maintain a certain standard of living for yourself and your children. I have this panicky feeling we're going to lose everything and be out on the streets. It feels pretty bad."

Anne blew her nose.

"Whatever happened to commitment?" Marilyn asked. "I mean, I thought when you got married, it was for better or worse. I thought you stuck it out to the end and tried. I thought you went to church and prayed together and loved each other and forgave each other and made it work. Then everybody started having affairs and getting divorces and having mid-life crises. Whoever heard of a mid-life crisis when we were growing up? Did they just invent that?" Marilyn was becoming irate.

"My parents didn't have the best marriage," she continued, "but they stayed together and I think they're happier than the couples I know who have gotten divorces and left the wives torn between jobs and children and poverty. We lost it someplace. I don't know where, but we lost it as a generation. It's a different world now. You better get yourself a lawyer, honey, and get Hugh before he gets you.

Because it's a rough life. And if you don't fight, you're going to get squashed."

To Anne, all of the choices were horrors. She went home depressed and bewildered. The message light on her home answering machine was blinking.

"Anne, this is Dave," the recording said. "I've worked out my schedule, and I'm flying to Fort Lauderdale tomorrow morning. I'll let you know what happens."

Chapter 7

Black Hole

Dave scanned faces in the crowd in the Fort Lauderdale-Hollywood International Airport, looking for Hugh. Indifferent eyes met his, then glanced away. He could not find the familiar face of his brother. After getting his luggage, Dave took a cab for Hugh's dockside condominium.

The cab shot along Fort Lauderdale's streets, streets lined with buildings sheathed with whiteness in the glare of the summer afternoon sun. As the cab pulled into Hugh's condominium complex, Dave caught a glimpse of a canal and boats between the buildings.

Dave rang the doorbell, waited, and rang it again. The door opened a wide crack. Dave could see Hugh in the dim light inside, dressed in a T-shirt and shorts.

"You're here," Hugh said.

"Yes. This is Friday, remember?"

"Yea. I just lost track of time. Come in," Hugh said, extending his hand. Dave grasped it. It felt cold.

Dave followed Hugh into the darkened condominium. Drapes over the sliding glass doors were drawn and fastened with clothespins to keep out slivers of light. Clothes lay abandoned on the floor. A dank smell emerged from somewhere.

"I'm glad you came," Hugh said. Dave had difficulty telling if he meant it. The fire seemed to have gone out of Hugh.

"I'm glad you want me to be here," Dave said. "That makes all the difference. Where do I put my things?"

"Oh," Hugh said, just noticing the suitcase Dave was carrying. "You can sleep in there." He pointed to the spare bedroom.

Dave carried his suitcase into the room and laid it flat on the bare mattress. He moved slowly, absorbing the condition of his brother. Hugh had lost his usual bravado, and now appeared almost...humiliated. Dave parted the curtains in the guest room and peered out the window at the canal and boats. Moisture laden with salt and dirt had collected on the outside of the window panes. Inside the room, once-lush plants had dropped their leaves on the beige carpet, leaving bare stems sticking out of the pots. A damp towel lay in a heap just inside the bedroom door. Newspapers and magazines lay on the floor in cluttered piles along the walls. On the top of the chest of drawers a paper cup and hamburger wrapper lay side by side. In the cup, leftover iced tea was covered with mold, and on the wrapper lay a piece of bun and bit of hamburger, the forgotten remains of an absent-minded meal. Beside these was a loose pile of outdated lottery tickets.

So, Hugh had been reduced to squalor within this luxury, Dave thought.

It was late afternoon. Dave went to the refrigerator and asked Hugh, "Okay if I have a coke?"

"Sure, let me see what I have."

In the refrigerator were a few items--some margarine, some milk, three soft drinks, part of a six-pack of beer askew in its plastic collar, a celery stalk wilted into a soft curl... Dave took out a soft drink and opened it.

"Want one?"

"Yea, I guess so."

Dave opened a soft drink for Hugh, too, and took a half-empty bag of pretzels from the counter. He sat in a stuffed chair.

"So, how's it been going?" Dave asked.

"Okay."

"Okay as in 'I'm doing okay for the shape I'm in?'"

"Yea, I guess something like that."

"What kind of shape are you in?"

"Pretty bad, I guess. I'm in deep shit, really, Dave. Sorry I didn't make it to the airport. Guess I slept through. How'd you get here?"

"Took a taxi."

"Sorry. I should have picked you up."

"It's okay. I can get around on my own. Let's get some supper, then we can talk."

After supper at a chain restaurant, Hugh sat on the edge of the sofa, his shirttail out, his clothes looking like they had been slept in.

"Now, tell me about it," Dave said.

"Not much to tell, I guess. I just can't seem to get myself moving. All I want to do is sleep. I have headaches almost every afternoon. I think I must have a virus or something, but I don't have any fever that I can tell. I think I'm going crazy."

"I think you're depressed."

"Yea, I am." Hugh leaned forward and put his head in his hands. He paused in silence for a long moment.

"I was in love with this woman, but she dumped me," he said, his eyes closed and his head down. "It really hurt. She got upset with me because I took another woman out. It was all my fault. I shouldn't have done it." Hugh heaved and began to cry into his hands. Dave waited for him to regain control.

"She really hurt you."

"Yes, but it was my fault. I hurt her first," Hugh said, wiping his face with the palm of his hand. "I was careless."

"You still love her."

"I'd take her back in a minute if she'd come."

"Was that Brenda Jacobs?"

"How'd you know about her?" Hugh leaned back in a slouch. Dave handed him a paper napkin to wipe his eyes.

"Her name was in the Charlotte paper in an article about your boat being confiscated."

"Oh, yes. No. She was the one I took out that one time. The woman I was in love with was Margo Hutchinson from Charlotte. I've known her about a year, and I loved her so much." Hugh wiped his face with the napkin.

"Hugh, what about Anne?"

Hugh flinched. "I know. I guess I've just pushed Anne out of the picture. I'm afraid I've hurt her pretty bad. I've been on a fling, and now I've crashed. I've made a big mess of things."

Dave thought for a moment.

"You can come out of this, Hugh. This doesn't have to be the end of the world," Dave said.

"I'm not so sure."

"You can get through this."

"My career is in a mess. I don't have any leads on a position and I can't get myself moving to try to find one. I think I'm going crazy."

"Like Dad?"

"I hope not."

"Do you think it was an accident?" Dave asked.

"Mom thinks so. She said it was an accident."

"What do you think?"

"I've thought it might have been suicide, but Mom was so sure it wasn't."

"It never quite made sense to me that the gun could have gone off accidentally," Dave said. "Dad was more careful than that."

"Do we have to talk about it?" Hugh said.

"Have you thought about killing yourself?"

"Yes."

"How much?"

"Quite a bit, I suppose."

"Have you thought about how you would do it?"

"Yes."

"How?"

"With a gun, I think."

"Do you have a gun?"

"Yes."

"Hugh, you have to promise me you won't kill yourself."

"I'm not sure I can do that."

"You have to."

"Okay."

"Okay what?"

"I won't kill myself."

"Good. Give me the gun."

"I said I wouldn't kill myself."

"You don't need the gun."

"Okay, but it's on the boat."

"Then, I'll get it later. You can come out of this, Hugh. You have a lot of good life ahead of you."

"You think so?"

"Yep."

"Maybe so."

The next morning, they went for a ride on Hugh's boat. Hugh cranked the engines and Dave released the lines. Hugh nosed the white Cigarette boat out into the canal at idle speed, moving toward the Intracoastal Waterway. A large marina lay on the left of the canal with boats tied to piers. A grey Florida Marine Patrol boat entered the canal just as they left it.

"The police are everywhere," Hugh said. "You have to be very careful to go slow in the no-wake zones or they'll pull you. They're looking for drug smugglers, mainly."

Out in the Intracoastal Waterway another grey patrol boat cruised slowly toward the 17th Street Bridge. Hugh fell in on the flank of the patrol boat and motored slowly under the bridge into the Port Everglades turning basin. Boat traffic was heavy. When they passed the end of the no-wake zone, Hugh pushed the throttles forward and put the boat on a plane headed for the Port Everglades inlet. The water roughened into steep four-foot waves in the inlet where the outgoing tidal current met the breeze. Hugh held on to a handle and braced his feet to meet the roll. They passed a small whaler plunging slowly toward the sea with a frightened looking couple aboard wearing life jackets. The whaler dropped six feet off the wake of Hugh's boat and slammed into the trough with a crash. Dave watched as the whaler turned and headed back toward the calm of the harbor. A third Florida patrol boat passed them coming into the inlet, followed by a Coast Guard boat, whose helmsman glared at Hugh.

"Right over there is where I ran aground," Hugh said above the noise of the waves and engines as he pointed to the left at a spot near a marker post. "I didn't know which side of the post to go on, and I guessed wrong."

When the boat reached a red buoy on the left about one mile out, Hugh turned northward and the waves subsided to a calmer level. On the left, the white beach stretched for miles ahead, framed by the skyline of multi-story hotels. A parasail boat towed a rider high above the water in front of the beach. Sunbathers spread their towels and applied sun tan lotion.

"Where's your gun?" Dave asked above the noise of the engines and wind.

"In the hanging locker down below."

Dave went into the cabin and emerged in a few minutes with a tactical-style pump shotgun.

"This is quite a weapon, Hugh."

"You need something like that against the AR-15s the drug smugglers have."

Dave held the gun over the seaward side of the boat, then dropped it into the water.

"That cost me four hundred and fifty dollars, you know?" Hugh said.

"Tough shit. Since when have you worried about money?"

The boat ran up the coast for a few miles with the throttles open, throwing necklace after necklace of diamond-sparkling spray into the ocean as Hugh drove her through the waves.

Then he turned the boat back toward the Port Everglades Inlet, this time careful to run out to the sea buoy before attempting to enter the inlet.

Back in the calm of the no-wake zone approaching the 17th Street Bridge, Dave said, "Are you ready to come back to Charlotte?"

"I'd like to, but I don't think I can face Anne right now."

"You could rent an apartment, stay on your own for a while, get your bearings. I could help you."

"That might be the way to go."

"I think it would be a good first step."

"I could always come back here if I wanted to."

"Yep."

"Yea, I guess it's the thing to do."

"Good. We'll pack up your stuff."

During the rest of that day, Dave helped Hugh prepare to leave. They tied up the Cigarette boat securely, using spring lines to allow it to rise and fall with the tide. Hugh bought a blue plastic tarpaulin to put over the Corvette. Dave washed dishes and clothes and tried to clean up the condominium.

Hugh packed his clothes in the leather suitcase he had bought so many weeks before, and on a humid, hazy morning, they loaded their things into the Porsche. Hugh turned to look once more at his things: the Cigarette boat in its slip, soggy with morning dew, a border of drab marine algae growing around its water line; the Corvette, looking disheveled under the blue tarp like a playboy under bed covers the morning after; the condominium, its balcony bare without the lush plants sported by so many other balconies. He felt that he had lost the game.

Dave drove first, steering the Porsche through downtown morning traffic to the Interstate 95 junction. Once on the interstate, Dave hit the speed limit and cruised northward in moderately light traffic, settling in to the usual interstate routine. They would break the long trip by spending the night at Savannah before turning onto Interstate 26 near Charleston and then Interstate 77 at Columbia which would take them to Charlotte.

The next day, as they drew close to Charlotte, Hugh felt his stomach tighten. Everything that he had left behind now came back into his consciousness with assault force. He hoped he wouldn't run into any of his former colleagues from Fortress. Thoughts of Anne flashed into his mind with sparks of panic. His only reprieve lay in the fact that Dave had invited him to stay at his house for a few days until he could make some other arrangements.

Hugh, alone, drove his Porsche slowly along the street of his dreams past, looking once again at the huge brick houses become unfamiliar in his absence. His chest tightened as he approached his house. He had phoned. Anne was waiting inside for him, waiting for their first meeting since he had left seven weeks ago. He swung into the driveway and stopped the car. Slowly, he opened the door and got out. His first impulse was to go to the front door, as though he weren't part of this family any more, but instead he walked to the back.

He rang the bell. Anne opened the door slowly. The inside of the house was dim. Anne looked out at him with a grey expression as though she were looking into a tomb.

"Hello, Anne," he said. The words fell at his feet. She swung the door open wide and stepped back, turning toward the inner part of the house.

Hugh opened the glass storm door and entered, holding the door behind him to allow it to close softly. He saw Anne, in the den, sit on the sofa. Hugh left the back door open and walked into the den after her. He sat on the edge of a stuffed chair.

"Anne?" he broke the silence.

She looked at him with a dull expression, as though he were a world removed from her.

"Anne, I'm sorry."

She closed her eyes slowly, then reopened them.

"What happened?" she asked.

"I went off on a tear, I guess."

"Do you have any idea what you've put us through?"

"A lot, I guess."

"A lot." Anne said the words flatly, evaluating them. "That doesn't quite cover it."

"Anne, I said I was sorry."

"Right. I just want you to know what you're sorry for, and I don't think you do."

"I know I hurt you."

She looked at him, nodding her head almost imperceptibly, angry.

Hugh looked down and shook his head, breaking her gaze. "Look, I don't know what we can do to get started again. I don't want to go over everything that happened. Can't we just put it behind us and go on from here?"

"I do want to go over everything that happened," Anne said. "I want you to know what you did to us. I want to know where you went and what you did and who you did it with."

"Anne...what's the point?"

"The point is that you destroyed our world when you left here. The point is you shattered our family. The point is you put us through hell. Is that enough? Is that enough of a point for you to consider going over it with me and taking responsibility for what you've done? Is that enough?" Anne was screaming through tears.

Hugh sat silent, paralyzed by the outburst of emotion.

"Okay, we'll go over it."

"Why did you leave us without saying a word?"

"It seems like so long ago, it's hard to remember."

"Well, try!"

"I just didn't feel good when I was here. I felt dragged down. Life wasn't exciting here."

"So you ran off and had an affair for excitement?"

"Anne...it's not so simple. I was having an affair already."

"Before you left?"

"Yes."

"With whom?"

"I won't tell you her name."

"Does she live in Charlotte?"

"Yes, she lives here. I met her at a seminar."

"Great. Was she Brenda Jacobs?"

"No."

"Who was Brenda Jacobs?"

"A woman I met in Florida."

"Did you have an affair with her?"

"Not much."

"What does that mean?"

"I just took her out once."

"She was arrested on your boat."

"That was the one time I took her out. But she wasn't arrested. I was charged with possession of marijuana, but it was her marijuana."

Anne sat silent for a moment.

"Were there any other women?"

"No."

"Two women." Anne's face wrinkled and she began to cry. After a few moments, she leaned back in the sofa and wiped her eyes with a tissue.

"Where are the girls?" Hugh asked.

"At Sally's. When you telephoned, I called her to see if she could keep them a while. She's been a good friend through all this."

They were silent for a moment, then Anne asked,

"Are you still seeing this woman in Charlotte?"

"No."

"When was the last time you saw her?"

"It's been several weeks ago."

"Are you finished with her?"

"Yes."

"Did you sleep with her?"

"Yes."

"Very often?"

"Fairly."

"Where did you sleep with her?"

"At her condominium, mostly."

"And you told me you were working late?"

"Yes."

"How could you?" Anne asked in hurt and anger, her eyes swollen and her face blotchy with dark areas.

Hugh sat silent.

"I trusted you," Anne said.

"I just got caught up in it," he said.

Anne stared at him in anger and disbelief.

"How much money did you spend, Hugh?"

"A lot."

"A lot. You like that expression, don't you? What all did you buy?"

"The boat. The condominium. A car."

"You had a nice car."

"I know. This was a Corvette. I'd always wanted one."

"How much did all that cost?"

"About a million one. But I can get most of that back if I want to."

"Ohhh," Anne groaned. "What happened, Hugh?"

"I guess I was flying a little high."

"Were you using drugs?"

"Not really. Once in a while."

"It's hard to understand."

"I know."

Anne shook her head.

"What else did you do?"

"That's about it."

"What about a job?"

"I don't have anything right now."

"Can you go back to Fortress?"

"I don't think so."

"Are you going to start over?"

"Yea, somewhere."

Anne shook her head again.

"When you left, Hugh, I felt the deepest hurt I've ever felt. I told the children that you'd gone away on business, but after a while I had to tell them you'd left us. Then I kept discovering bits and pieces of information about what you were doing. The credit card bills came. The statement from the investment account came. The newspaper had that article about your boat being confiscated with that woman on board and you being charged with possession of marijuana. It was like you were some stranger I didn't know. I thought you'd gone crazy."

"I'm sorry I put you through that, Anne."

"It still doesn't seem believable. It seems like it didn't really happen, like it was just a weird dream. Did it really happen, Hugh?"

"I'm afraid so."

"Why?"

"I just felt so good. It's hard to explain. It was like a drug, and I wanted to keep it going. I know it's not rational."

"Well, it certainly didn't feel good to me."

"I know."

"What are you going to tell the children?"

"I don't know."

"I think you'd better apologize to them."

"I could do that."

"I think you need to. This hasn't been good for them."

"I'm sorry."

Hugh looked around at the den and the kitchen.

"The house looks good," he said.

"I've tried."

"Anne, I want to come back home," Hugh said.

"Not now. Not yet. I'm not ready for that."

"Dave will let me stay for a few days. I'll have to get an apartment after that, if I can't come home."

"I just can't have you here yet."

"Okay. I understand."

They fell silent.

"I guess I'll be going" Hugh said. "Can we talk again soon?"

"Yea. I don't look forward to it, but I guess we'll have to."

"I'd like to see the kids."

"Maybe next time."

Hugh walked to the back door and out into the car port.

Anne closed the door tightly, as though doing so would shut out the pain.

Chapter 8

Interface

Pain accompanied Anne to bed that night after Hugh had left the house. She awoke at 2:30 a.m. and felt anger rising in her, bristling and pricking inside, filling her like hot water rising in a tank. She swung out of bed, put on her slippers and robe, walked by the children's rooms hoping to catch a calm feeling of love to counteract the burning inside, and settled into a chair with a book in the den. But instead of reading, she thought. Two women...their faces blurry...naked breasts pressing against her Husband Hugh...a kiss. Why? How? How much had he cared for them? What could motivate a man so strongly that it would lead him to cause such damage? What had these women looked like? How aggressive had they been? Why hadn't it always been her? She felt violated.

Pain carried Anne to Dave's office the next morning while Elizabeth and Angie were at their schools. She sat across the desk from him.

"Hugh wants to come back home, you know?" she said.

"I know. He told me."

"I'm not sure. I just don't think I'm ready for that."

"What are your feelings toward Hugh right now?"

"I hate him. I'm furious at him. I think what he did was horrible. I don't understand how he could do what he did. I don't understand how he could hurt someone he loved the way he hurt me. I'm not sure he really loves me anymore. He had that affair, you know, maybe two, and he spent a lot of our money. I don't think he knows what he put us through when he left."

"He knows he hurt you, but he hasn't been through what you've been through."

"No, he hasn't. And now he wants to move back in, just like that, like nothing ever happened."

"It's going to take time."

"A lot of time. I'm not sure I can ever get over this."

"It depends on whether you'll be able to forgive him. If you can't forgive him, you probably won't be able to go on together. If you can, you'll carry some scars, but you might be able to make it as a couple. I think forgiveness is the right thing, but forgiving him won't be easy."

"I don't know if I can do it."

"An old professor of mine said, the one who forgives takes it. The one who forgives pays a price."

"If I felt like he were really taking responsibility for what he did, it would help."

"What does he say?"

"He says he's sorry."

"That sounds encouraging."

"Yes, but I don't think he knows how sorry he needs to be. I don't think he knows how much pain he caused."

"He might not, and he might not ever realize that."

"For weeks I wished he were back home, and now that he's back, I'm not sure I want him. I'm not sure I know him anymore. I'm not sure I can love him."

"Do you love him at all?"

"Yes. Underneath I think I still love him. I don't know why."

"Maybe you can stick with him, then. Give yourself some time to sort things out. I'd like to see you two stay together."

"I think we could use some counseling."

"Yea, that could really help."

"Could you do it?"

"I'm not sure I'm the best choice since I'm Hugh's brother."

"I think he would come to you, and I'm not sure he would go to anybody else."

"I'll consider doing it. Whether you come to me for marriage counseling or not, I want to try to get Hugh to go to a psychiatrist. I think he may be having some biochemical problems."

"What do you mean?"

"He may have a chemical imbalance in his central nervous system that causes his moods to swing dramatically."

"Have you mentioned this to Hugh?"

"No. I didn't want to hit him with it too soon."

"He won't like the idea of going to a psychiatrist, I can tell you that."

"That's true. But if he's hurting enough, he'll do it."

"I think it's a great idea myself."

"We'll give it a try."

"When are you going to tell him?"

"I'll see how he's feeling tonight. Maybe then."

"Let me know how that goes."

"I will."

"If he would go to a psychiatrist and we could get some counseling, I might be able to go on with the marriage."

"I think it would be a tremendous help to Hugh and to your marriage."

"What a mess. Why do these things have to happen? Everything was going along so well, and then, boom."

"I know what you mean."

"Do you think we'll make it?"

"I think you'll both make it. Whether you make it as a couple, I don't know. I hope so."

"I hope so, too. I'd like to."

"Good. Let's work in that direction."

Anne left Dave's office and drove to Sally Sterling's house. She felt relieved to think her marriage might survive, but this didn't remove the hurt over what Hugh had done to her. How do I know Hugh won't do this again? she asked herself. And that was the question she posed Sally when they were seated at the kitchen table over cups of coffee.

"You don't," Sally said. "But if he does, either shoot him or divorce him."

"You're kidding, aren't you?"

"Not really. I've seen how badly he's hurt you and the girls, and I wouldn't want to see you hurt again."

"I would sure feel like shooting him."

"You probably feel like it now."

"Sometimes."

"Have you thought seriously about divorcing him?"

"Yes, but I don't really want to."

"Maybe you better think about your options. How are you going to overlook what Hugh's done?"

"I really can't overlook it."

"So how are you going to get over it?"

"I'm hoping we can work through it."

"That won't be easy, Anne."

"I know, but divorce is painful, too."

"That's true. You know Marilyn Arrington's going back to court, don't you?"

"No. Why?"

"She's suing Trot for some money he owes her. It's not that much, three thousand dollars or so, but he refuses to pay. Marilyn says she'll get it because he's in contempt of court for not paying it."

"Uhnn," Anne groaned.

"But I'm afraid it's worse than that. Trot has a live-in girlfriend now, and they throw a lot of wild parties. When the children are with him, they're exposed to all that. Marilyn said the children come back with all kinds of wild tales. Trot and his girlfriend make out in front of the kids when they're watching television, and they don't hide their lovemaking. And when they have parties, people get drunk and smoke pot and disappear into bedrooms. The kids retreat to their rooms, but they can't get away from it. Then, when they come home to Marilyn's, they have all these wild ideas about staying up late and getting anything they want and calling her by her first name. It's really hard for Marilyn."

"It must be hard for the children, too, going back and forth between two different value systems. What values are they supposed to think are right?" Anne said.

"I know. I feel like Trot is mistreating the children. And he sends messages to Marilyn through them. It's pretty bad."

"How can a relationship that promises life's greatest security turn into one that brings violence to your inner being? How can your most intimate companion suddenly become your intimate enemy?" Anne said.

"I don't know. It makes you believe that old bumper sticker that says, 'Shit Happens.' Those who have been shit on sure believe it."

"Yea, but there's more to it than that. Marilyn said the lawyers make couples into enemies, but they couldn't if the laws didn't allow it. And you have to go back to the individuals involved, too. If Hugh hadn't committed adultery, I wouldn't be so hurt and have to decide whether to divorce him or shoot him or forgive him. We're morally adrift. We've lost touch with the values that held us together without our realizing it."

"There sure is a lot of loose sex these days."

"The liberation morality has dumped us into the old immorality. We're learning from hard experience what our parents and grandparents learned from their faith. There are reasons for moral rules, and when people break the rules they turn life into hell for themselves and everybody else."

"Yea, but I'm not sure I want to go back to the old Victorian ways, either," Sally said.

"Well, I don't either, but there's got to be a happy medium. There are so many divorces we have a whole generation of children growing up with one parent. Who knows what that will do to them? We've concentrated a lot of energy on correcting social wrongs and helping the poor and keeping the environment clean, but we've let go of the personal moral values that it turns out were important after all. That's why Trot and Marilyn are killing each other. That's why Hugh and I have such a massive problem to solve. And this is multiplied by thousands, millions of couples, all over the country, all over the world. Think of the pain! Can you see the enormity of the pain this generates?"

"Yes, but this has been happening for centuries. Immorality is nothing new."

"But the scope of it is new. It always happened, and always will, I suppose, but not this much of it."

"So, what do you do about it?"

"I'm not going to be defeated by this. I'm not going to let this garbage destroy my life. We entered into a marriage covenant, and I'm going to keep my part if I can be sure Hugh is going to try to keep his part."

"That'll be tricky. How can you be sure he'll try?"

"We need to do a lot of talking."

"Have you thought about counseling?"

"Yes. And I've talked with Dave about it. I think it would really help, and if Hugh would get counseling with me, and if I had some assurance that he wouldn't take off on a wild flight again, I might be able to go ahead with the marriage. Right now, Hugh wants to come back home, and I have to decide whether to let him."

"How do you feel about it?"

"I don't know. I'm so angry at him I don't want to be around him. Sometimes I feel like I'm going to explode, and I don't think that would do either of us any good. It might only drive us apart. I need some time to sort through all this. I think it would be better if we aren't around each other all day for a while. I need the space. I have a lot of strong feelings to work through."

"What else are you feeling?"

"Pain. It just hurts so much, and I don't want to hurt any more. I hurt terribly after Hugh left, but then I started to get over it. Now that he's back, I'm hurting all over again."

"You've really been through the wringer."

"I'm so uncertain about Hugh. I can't trust him anymore. I'm not sure he's settled down. I'd like to know he means to stay committed to the marriage if he comes home again and we try to work through all this."

"That's going to be hard to know ahead of time. You might have to let him come home for a while before you can get a feeling for where Hugh is."

"I'm afraid you're right," Anne said, shaking her head.

"It won't be easy," Sally said.

"Nope."

The two women fell silent for a moment as Sally opened a box of bakery oatmeal cookies.

"I just flip flop, Sally. One minute I feel positive about getting back together, and the next minute I'm scared to death."

"Does Hugh act like he's sorry?"

"He says he's sorry. He didn't want to talk about what he had done at first, but he did when I pushed. I don't think he wants to look at his guilt too much."

"That would be hard for him, but I agree he has to own up to what he's done. He's really done some wild things, and he's dumped on you royally. Maybe you and the girls are better off without him. You could get a big settlement since he has so much money, and you could probably get a lot of child support."

"I don't know. I've got to think about it. I took a marriage vow, you know. I promised to love him in joy and sorrow and sickness and health 'till death do us part."

"What about in adultery and wastefulness? What do the vows say about those?"

"It's bad, I admit it. But I don't want to just dump him."

"What if he does it again?"

"I couldn't handle that. I'd have to get out."

"At least you're not being foolish."

Dave and Hugh sat in Dave's warm, modest den after supper one evening. Lamps set the darkened pine paneling aglow and framed the leather-colored furniture in which they were sitting with reddish light. A gun rack on the wall held an antique hunting piece. A rack full of pipes sat on a table under one of the lamps, though Dave had given up smoking several years before. Along one wall were shelves full of books. On another wall was a flat screen television and a set of large speakers.

"I'm not going to any shrink. I don't need that," Hugh told Dave when he broached the subject to him.

"You're depressed as hell. You've been off on a tear that has wrecked your life. You can't get yourself moving. I think you need professional help."

"There's nothing wrong with me," Hugh said.

"Then why can't you get it all together?"

"I will. I will. Just give me time. The old spark will come back."

"Yea, it will come back, and you'll take off like a rocket ship and still have all of your problems."

"When I'm feeling good, I don't have any of these problems."

"But you do, Hugh. You just don't realize it. You'll be right back in a jam again, only by then Anne will have divorced you and you'll have a bigger set of problems to deal with."

Hugh was silent.

"I've watched you, Hugh. I've seen you soar and I've seen you crash. This is not the first time. It's happened over and over again. Remember how depressed you were your junior year in college? Remember how you got in trouble for cheating? Remember the week when you just disappeared and everybody was looking for you? This is nothing new, Hugh. I think something else is going on inside that needs to be dealt with."

"Like what? You think I'm insane? You think I belong in a mental institution?"

"I think you have a chemical imbalance."

"What?"

"Some people have an imbalance in the chemicals in their central nervous system that causes them to have mood swings. Their moods go real high, and then they go real low. It doesn't mean they're crazy. It just means that their systems aren't functioning right."

"There's nothing wrong with my central nervous system."

"There might be, Hugh, and if there is, the treatment for it is very simple. They just give you some medication."

"Tranquilizers?"

"Not tranquilizers."

"What then?"

"I'm not a doctor, Hugh. You need a doctor to tell you this sort of thing. But they would probably give you antidepressants or lithium."

"Can't you get addicted to that stuff?"

"No, they're not addictive, no more than insulin is for a diabetic. It's just something that the system needs to correct the chemical imbalance."

"I don't know, Dave. I just don't want to go to a shrink and get into all that."

"Well, I think you need to, and I think it could help you a lot, not just for now but for the rest of your life."

Hugh shook his head.

"Think about it," Dave said.

Angie, watching out the dining room window, saw Hugh's Porsche turn into the driveway.

"Daddy's here!" she yelled into the house, and, turning from the window, she ran into the den leaving the sheer curtains flying.

Anne caught her as Angie ran into the den.

"Want to go meet him?" she said, turning the little girl toward the kitchen door.

Elizabeth hung back by the den door, less enthusiastic.

"Elizabeth, you coming?" Anne asked her. It would be the first time the girls had seen their father since his return.

The older girl dropped her head and went.

Hugh walked into the garage where Angie met him with a hug around the leg.

"Hello, Angel Pie, how ya' doin'?" Hugh said, picking her up.

"I missed you, Daddy," she said. "You were gone a long time!"

"I know, honey. I missed you too."

"Hello, Hugh," Anne said. She had walked out into the garage behind Angie.

"Hey, Anne. How you doin'?" Hugh said.

Elizabeth stood in the kitchen door, staring at him, holding on to the door frame. Hugh saw her and put Angie down.

"Elizabeth! Hello," Hugh said.

"Hi, Daddy," she said, and dropped her eyes.

"It's good to see you," Hugh said.

"It's good to see you, too," Elizabeth said. "I thought you weren't coming back."

"Sure I was coming back. You didn't think I'd just go off forever, did you?"

"I thought you had."

"Nah. I was coming back."

"You stayed a long time."

"Yea, but I'm back now."

"Why aren't you living with us anymore?"

"Well, your mommy and I just have to work some things out. I'll be back soon. You'll see."

Elizabeth took him by the hand, turned, and led him into the den with his left arm over her right shoulder. Angie raced around them and jumped onto the couch with a bounce. Hugh and Elizabeth sat on the couch, too, with one daughter on each side of their father. Anne sat in the stuffed chair, a concerned look on her face.

"Daddy, come look at my drawings," Angie said, jumping down from the couch and pulling Hugh's left hand.

"I just sat down, Honey."

"But come look, Daddy," Angie said, pulling hard.

Hugh yielded and let the little girl lead him back to her room.

"See, Daddy. Do you like them?"

Before him on the wall were several drawings, the most prominent of which was a crayon drawing of a house. It was the likeness of their own house, which one could tell by the red brick and two storeys. In the front yard were three stick figures in skirts, a woman and two girls, side by side. A green tree with a brown trunk stood on the right side of the house, a yellow sun shone down from the middle, and in the upper left corner floating tilted in the sky was the stick figure of a man.

"I didn't know where you were, so I put you up there," Angie said.

"It's very nice," Hugh said.

A delighted Angie ran back into the den squealing and jumped on the couch.

Hugh felt suddenly sad and turned to leave Angie's room quickly.

"So, how have you been doing?" Anne asked Hugh in the den.

"Okay. I'm starting to look for an apartment."

"Any luck?"

"Not yet. How about letting me come home."

"Girls, go to your rooms and play. Daddy and I want to talk," Anne said.

The girls slid off the couch and headed for their rooms.

"What do you think?" Hugh asked.

"I'm still not ready for that. I think we should get some counseling."

"Okay. You want to see if Dave will do it?"

"Yes, that would be my choice. Could you go to him for counseling? He is your brother."

"Yes, I could do that."

"Dave said he thought you should go to a psychiatrist."

"He told me."

"Are you going?"

"I don't need a psychiatrist. I'm fine. I'm not a weirdo."

"Dave said you might have a chemical imbalance."

"There's nothing wrong with my brain chemistry, and I'm not going to a damned shrink to have him probe into my unconscious mind looking for something. I just don't need it."

"You put us through pure hell, Hugh, and I am not going down that road again. I'm willing to try to go on with the relationship, but not if you're going to fly off on one of these affairs again. Can you understand that? I'm having a hard time trusting you, Hugh, and it will take some doing to restore that trust. Dave says this might help, and I think it's worth a try. If you don't get some professional help, I don't think I can go on with this relationship."

"Terrific. That's going to look great on a resume, 'History of mental illness.'"

"You can cross that bridge when you come to it. Right now you need to get your act together."

"That's the way it is, huh?"

"That's the way it is. You hurt us, Hugh."

"Revenge."

"No. I just don't want it to happen again."

Hugh stood up. "Well, I'm leaving," he said.

"Leaving here, or leaving me?"

"I haven't decided yet."

"Well, I hope you'll consider going to the doctor."

"I'll think about it. Tell the girls 'Bye' for me," Hugh said, and he walked out the kitchen door.

Chapter 9

Space Probe

Hugh sat in his Porsche in the parking lot of the Metroview Building, his head down, staring at the steering wheel. He hoped no one he knew would see him. In ten minutes, he had an appointment with Dr. Helen Rothschild, psychiatrist.

Headlines flashed through his mind: "Man who killed ten is under care of psychiatrist." He wondered if people would think of him as some kind of latent criminal. He hadn't wanted to come, in spite of Dave's talking to him, in spite of Anne's telling him if he didn't get help she wouldn't go on with the marriage. Even now, he thought he might just drive off and forget it. But, he had been very depressed. He stayed for days in his newly-found apartment and drank and slept. He didn't want to go on like this. He couldn't get himself moving to do anything.

Dave had recommended Dr. Rothschild to him, and Hugh had made the appointment. His mind flashed back to the conversation he had had with Dave.

"Does it bother you that you left Anne and had this affair?" Dave had asked.

"Yea, I feel guilty about it," Hugh said. "Sometimes I feel like the guilt will overwhelm me, will make me a worm who has no power or right to direct his own life but who has to submit to Anne forever."

"You won't have to do that, you know."

"Well, sometimes I feel like I have to. Now, on top of the guilt, I feel ashamed at having to go to a psychiatrist. The act of going to a psychiatrist creates a new problem in itself."

"Yes, I think it would be hard on your self-esteem."

"I feel like I'm about to give up my status as a self-directed person and become one of those people whose sick lives are determined by medicine. That thought makes me even more depressed! Once I give in to this help, once I admit I am made of the wrong stuff and offer myself up to be repaired, I am saying I am defective. Dave, I am about to become one of those people who require a psychiatrist whose job is to lock up poor mental patients in hospitals. It makes me wonder if I'm like them."

"I know it's not easy for you," Dave said. "But, you don't require hospitalization. You're not crazy. All you need from the psychiatrist is a diagnosis and perhaps some medication and counseling."

"Great. That's all, huh? And open myself to the contempt of the world? How will other investment people look at this? Will they still think my judgment is sound? Will they trust me to handle big accounts? Will I still be allowed to vote? Get a passport? Hold a driver's license?"

Dave started to speak, but Hugh interrupted him.

"I know. I'm being irrational. But that's how I feel! My emotions are screaming that I'm about to make a big mistake."

"You have to think about more than yourself, Hugh."

"I know. I've hurt Anne and the children, my own flesh and blood, and they didn't deserve it and it shouldn't happen again if I can help it. I guess I have to do this. I guess I have to sentence myself to this, turn myself in to the authorities and undergo this humiliation."

Hugh sounded bitter.

"Try to look at this situation objectively," Dave offered. "If going to a psychiatrist will help you live with a circumstance you can't control, it's good and you should do it."

"Yea, but I hate it. I hate admitting I have any inherent flaws."

"What are your choices?"

"I guess I have two choices--either go to the psychiatrist and possibly go on with this marriage, or leave Anne and go back to Florida."

Hugh sat in his Porsche outside the Metroview building and thought about Florida, about his boat, his condominium, his dream that lay molding beside a Fort Lauderdale canal. He thought about Anne and Elizabeth and Angie and their house and remembered the warmth that had been there, that he had never stopped to appreciate, that might still await him. Anne seemed set in her decision not to let him come home, and when she became set like that, Hugh knew that she would hold firm and not give in. He had succeeded in getting rich, but he had failed as a husband and father. Maybe it was time he did something about it.

He threw open the car door and bolted out--like jumping from an airplane.

The office was on the sixth floor. The small waiting room was tastefully decorated with a sofa and upholstered chairs. On the walls were framed Charleston prints. The receptionist, a youthful woman wearing a white blouse and gold chain necklace, sat at a counter behind a glass window. He went to her and said, "I'm Hugh Packard. I have an appointment with Dr. Rothschild." Then he sat in an upholstered chair away from the others in the waiting room to fill out a form she had given him.

Over the top of the form, Hugh studied the other people in the room. A pretty, middle-aged woman sat in a chair gripping an open magazine. Across from her, a teen-aged girl in rumpled jeans slumped across the sofa with one leg over an armrest, looking peeved. In another chair, an overweight, dumpy woman with a tired, sagging face sat staring into space. Beside her, an unshaven, wrinkled man wearing a striped shirt with the sleeves rolled up and fingering an unlit cigarette turned the pages of a magazine. Hugh felt uncomfortable. Who knew what storms were raging in these people's heads? He wondered.

He read and waited, sorted through the stack of magazines looking for something of interest, and thought. He had believed since his father's death that a person had to play the hand he was dealt. There was no use making excuses, no use blaming circumstances for failure. One simply had to take what one was given and within that framework try to succeed. He had never allowed the tragedy of his father's early death be an excuse for his failures. If his father's death set him behind others who were not similarly handicapped, he would simply have to take that into consideration and try harder. He couldn't change his personal history. So now, if he did have a chemical imbalance, and he thought maybe Dave was right that he did, he had to accept that as a part of the hand dealt to him and do the best he could, given that limitation.

An attractive, well-dressed woman of about 40 opened the door into the waiting room. "Hugh Packard?" she said to Hugh.

Hugh nodded and put down the magazine he was holding.

"You can come on back."

Helen Rothschild was wearing a fashionable green plaid suit with a white, open-neck blouse. Hugh followed her down a hallway, noticing the smooth curve of her hips under her skirt, not yet sure if this were the doctor. She opened a door into another room and stood back for Hugh to enter first. The room looked like a small den, except that in it was a desk facing the wall with a chair and lamp. Books lined the wall behind the desk, and opposite it was a short cloth-covered sofa.

Hugh sat on the sofa and Dr. Rothschild sat in the chair at the desk. She had medium length, dark hair and an attractive, though not pretty, face. She wore a thick gold necklace and earrings, and her appearance was more like that to be found in a fashion magazine than in a clinic.

"What can I do for you?" she asked, crossing her legs. Hugh noticed the curve of her thigh as it disappeared into her skirt. This might not be so bad, Hugh thought.

"I've been having some problems," Hugh said.

"What kind of problems?"

"My brother..."

"That's Dave Packard, right?"

"Right. Dave thinks I have a chemical imbalance and suggested I come to you. Recently, I've been very depressed and can't get myself moving, but before that I felt great, so great I got myself into trouble."

"Tell me about it."

Hugh hesitated. This was sudden, and he wasn't sure he trusted her. But her unexpected seductiveness made him feel warm toward her. She was waiting, attentive to him.

"I quit my job," Hugh began. "I thought I was going to establish myself as a big investment trader in New York. I'd been working for Fortress Securities here in town and thought they were too conservative for me. So I left with the idea of doing bigger and better things. I felt great. I felt like I could do anything. But I felt dragged down by my wife and family, and I hated that feeling, so I went to Fort Lauderdale..."

"You left your family?"

"Yes. And I bought a condominium in Fort Lauderdale, right on the water near the port and the inlet, and I bought a boat like I had always wanted and a '61 Corvette. I had been having an affair with a woman here in Charlotte, and I flew her down to Florida whenever she would come. But we had a falling out, and then I crashed. She pulled the rug out from under me, and I just couldn't seem to bounce back. I tried everything. I drank a lot. I did some drugs."

"What kind of drugs?" Dr. Rothschild was taking notes. "Cocaine, marijuana," Hugh said, waiting for the look of censure.

"Okay. Go on," she said, as though he had said Coca Cola.

Hugh didn't know what else to say.

"Tell me about the falling out you had with this woman."

"I had taken out another woman," Hugh said. "It was nothing, just an afternoon lark, but we went out on my boat, and I ran aground, and the Coast Guard came and found a marijuana cigarette on my boat. It was her joint. And she had a bag of marijuana, too. But they confiscated my boat and charged me with possession of marijuana, and it made the newspapers all the way up here in Charlotte. So when Margo saw the papers--Margo is the woman I was in love with--she was upset that I had taken out this other woman, and she ended up dumping me."

"That hurt."

"Yes. It hurt terribly. I don't know when I've been so depressed."

"Have you seen Margo any more?"

"No."

"Okay. Go on."

"That's about it. I still haven't come out of it. Dave came down to Florida, and I decided to come back to Charlotte. I've seen my wife, Anne, and the kids, but she doesn't want me to come home yet. I'm not sure she ever will."

"Dave told me this is not the first time this kind of thing has happened to you. That's why he thinks you have a chemical imbalance. Is that right? And, by the way, Dave and I work together on a lot of cases and trust each other."

"Yes, this kind of thing has happened before. I feel great, super great, and then I fall into a black depression. I'm really very successful, you know. I've made a lot of money in stock options."

"But you swing real high and then you swing real low?"

"Yes."

"Can you tell if you do this on a regular schedule?"

"What do you mean?"

"Do you swing high and then low every month, or every six months, or every year, or every few years? Can you see a pattern?"

"I never thought about it. Let's see. It does seem that I feel good in the spring, and then about the beginning of summer I'm going great guns."

"And then you get depressed."

"Yes."

"Do you always get depressed afterwards?"

"Yes, I think so."

"Anybody else in your family do this? Brother, sister, mother, father?"

"My brother seems to be fine. My mother gets depressed, but she's had a hard life. My father died when I was young, so it's hard for me to know what he was like."

"What did he die of?"

"A gunshot wound."

Dr. Rothschild looked at Hugh.

"My mother says it was an accident that happened while he was cleaning his shotgun. I've never been sure. He was not the kind of person who would have been careless."

"Did he have any mood problems? Did he have mood swings?"

"I don't know."

"Was he an alcoholic?"

"He drank a lot, but no one ever said he was an alcoholic."

Dr. Rothschild took out a prescription pad.

"I'm going to try you on lithium," she said. "It won't hurt you to take it, and I think, given your family history and what you and Dave have said about your mood swing, it's fairly certain that you have manic-depressive disease. This is caused by a chemical imbalance in your central nervous system that causes your moods to swing very high and then very low." She drew a diagram showing a line that went up and down in waves.

"First, you go too high," she said, "and then too low. The lithium, which is actually lithium carbonate, is a simple compound which has a great track record for smoothing out the swings. It's not addictive, and you're not apt to feel anything sudden. But over the first couple of weeks after you start taking it, you should begin to come out of your depression. After that, things should go smoother. If not, we'll see then. We might add an antidepressant.

"This will take some of the height off your highs and some of the depth off your lows, but it will not stifle your energy. In fact, some people say it enhances their creativity because they are not driven so compulsively by their highs."

Hugh was stunned and simply sat there listening. His head spun. He hadn't expected to have her come to a conclusion so quickly, and he didn't like the idea of having to take the drug. The words "manic-depressive" stuck like a bone in his throat.

Dr. Rothschild handed him the prescription. "I want to see you again in two weeks," she said. And as though anticipating his thoughts, she added, "Don't get hung up on the technical terminology. You're not a maniac," and patted him on the back just above his hips as he walked out the door carrying the prescription. Her touch gave Hugh a warm, sexual shot. She saw to it that he had another appointment, then bid him good-bye as she disappeared back down the hallway. Hugh went out of the office and breathed deeply as he waited for the elevator.

I'll be damned if I'm going to take this drug, he said to himself. It's a crutch, and I don't need it. He rode the elevator down and went out to his Porsche. The beautiful workmanship of the car gave him a good feeling. He got in and started the powerful engine. It seemed whole and good. So, I'm manic-depressive, he thought. So, I have a defective brain. So, the hell with this.

He drove out of the parking lot and onto Randolph Road, heading for his apartment. He wanted a drink. He drove fast along the four-lane road, impatient with traffic. He cut into the right lane to avoid a slow car in front of him, barely making it in front of a pick-up truck already in the right lane. Then Hugh saw a car lunging into his lane from a side street. He swerved left just in time to miss the car, but the pick-up truck behind him slammed into the driver's door with a concussion that shook Hugh. Hugh's impulse was to drive on, but instead he made himself pull to the side of the road and run back.

He was the first to reach the smashed vehicles. The truck had come to rest a few feet from the crushed side of the car. The driver of the truck was climbing out. Hugh turned to the car and looked in. The sight horrified him. A man in his fifties was slumped over sideways in the pulverized driver's seat, the left side of his swollen head was smashed and bleeding, a piece of his skull protruding from the bloody pulp. Bits of glass covered everything.

Hugh turned away involuntarily and covered his eyes. He thought he would vomit. Other people came running up and looked into the smashed car. Hugh walked to his Porsche and got in behind the driver's seat. His hands were shaking. Soon, a police car arrived, followed quickly by an Emergency Medical Service ambulance. Hugh walked back to the accident, thinking he could tell the police what had happened. The paramedics were pulling the man out of the passenger's side of the car and putting him on a stretcher. Hugh looked at the man's face again, bloody and horrifying, and he saw his father. He saw his father as he lay on the floor in their home, saw through the eyes of a boy the holocaust that had fallen upon them, saw the ambulance drivers carry him out of their home, saw himself in his father's place.

No. Not me, he thought.

He gave his name and address to the policeman and, in a daze, told him what he had seen as the policeman took notes. Then he drove home and lay down on his bed. The sight of the man's crushed head kept returning to his mind, horribly, giving him a sense of panic. He remembered his father, his father's drinking, his long work absences, his distance. After resting, he drove to a drug store and handed the pharmacist the prescription. My life is going to be different, he thought. Then he returned to his apartment, took the first of the pills, and went to sleep.

After two weeks, Hugh began to be surprised that he felt better. In subtle ways, he realized that something was happening. He felt a tingling in his spine as he listened to music and realized that it was something he hadn't felt in a long time. Colors seemed more intense. Food tasted better. Speech came easier, and he remembered facts better. Thoughts of suicide came less frequently. Instead of dwelling on death, he began to sense life everywhere.

One night when he was carrying a plastic bag of garbage to the dumpster, he looked up at the stars. He hadn't looked up much recently, and he was struck by the sight. The night was clear, and he was standing in the darkness behind his apartment building. The sky was a dome of diamonds, a dazzling array of bright stars. The moon shone crisp like a half circle of sun-lit snow set against the velvet blackness of the cosmos. Hugh saw the dipper-like shape of Pegasus, familiar since his childhood, and he felt, mystically, at home in the universe.

Hugh's phone rang late one afternoon. It was Anne.

"I want to bring you something," she said.

"Sure, come on over."

"Don't eat supper yet. I'll be there in forty-five minutes."

When Hugh opened the door to her, he was greeted by wonderful aromas.

"I've brought you some food," she said, stepping past him into the apartment carrying a plate and a bowl covered with aluminum foil.

She set them on his kitchen table and removed the foil. Steam rose from a plate of baked chicken and a bowl of green beans with roasted almonds.

"I've got more," she said, leaving the apartment.

In a minute she returned with hot rolls, scalloped potatoes and half a pumpkin pie.

"This all looks great," Hugh said. "What got into you?"

"I fixed this for us and thought you might like some," she said.

"Well, sit down and eat with me," Hugh said.

"I've already eaten, but I'll stay for a little while and have dessert with you. The girls are over at Sally's spending the night."

Anne busied herself setting out the food while Hugh poured two glasses of wine.

"So, how have you been?" Anne asked.

"I've been doing well," Hugh said. "The lithium seems to be working. Dr. Rothschild wants me to keep taking the present dosage for a while, then she might taper it off. But, I've been feeling really good. I'm going to start looking for a job. I think I'll go to some of the other brokerage houses in town and see if they need someone."

"I guess you can't go back to Fortress."

"No. I wouldn't even try. It would be too humiliating."

"You look better. I can see it in your eyes. You look happier and more rested."

"Yea, I think I'm on the right track. I never would have believed that a drug could make such a difference in a person's thinking. I mean, I thought my philosophy of life was my own, a well thought-out cynicism developed over years of reading and contemplation. But now I'm thinking differently, I'm having different ideas about life, and I think it's because of the lithium. Suddenly there's a place for happiness in my scheme of things, and it wasn't there before. There was only a compulsively driven high or a black depression. Isn't that strange?

It's great! Why didn't somebody tell me about this before?"

"You'd never have listened before, for one thing. I can't believe you're happy about going to a psychiatrist."

"Well, I wouldn't say I'm happy about it, but if it works, I won't knock it."

Hugh dug ravenously into his plate of food.

"This is so good," he said. "It's the best food I've ever tasted."

"You're just hungry for home cooking," Anne said.

Anne watched Hugh as he scooped up the food.

"You really seem changed," she said.

"I feel different."

"Maybe we could try having you move back home for a while."

"Sounds good to me. Of course, I just got this apartment."

"You could keep it a while until we see how things work out."

"Well, I guess it's worth a try. What changed your mind?"

"Your willingness to go to the psychiatrist. The change in your attitude."

"It wasn't easy."

"I'm sure it wasn't."

"I'm still not all that comfortable with it, but I'll stay with it as long as it works."

"I'm glad."

"You know, I do love you. I haven't always shown it, but I do," Hugh said.

"I love you, too, in spite of all you have done. I find myself thinking about you and loving you. I hate you sometimes, too, though. I haven't gotten beyond that yet."

"Maybe there's hope for us."

"Maybe."

Hugh stood up, went to her, and kissed her. She pressed her lips against his in response. She stood up, and he embraced her.

"It's been a long time," she said.

"I know."

They kissed again. Hugh caressed her breast.

"Not yet," she said.

Hugh hugged her and rubbed her back and hips with his hands, lifting and loosening her skirt, then he kissed her again. He could feel through her skirt the smooth fabric of her panties. She felt warm and open toward him and pressed her thighs against his.

Hugh led her to his bedroom and they made love, sensing the novelty of strangeness mixed with the comfort of familiarity. Afterward, lying together, Anne felt awakened, new.

Chapter 10

Orbit

Anne set about the weekly cleaning of the house with an energy she hadn't felt in months. Hugh had come home, and while she still had mixed feelings about him, there was a chance the future would be rosier.

She put fresh sheets on the beds, emptied the waste baskets and vacuumed the entire house. Then she tackled the girls' rooms, hanging up clothes and putting away toys, straightening out curtains and hanging fresh towels in the bathrooms. She did this in spite of herself.

I'm a fool, she thought. Why am I working so hard for him? Are we women such idiots that we fall all over our men no matter how much they dump on us? Is there some female instinct that drives us to do this? I ought to kick him in the butt, but instead I'm making the house nice for him. Damn him! How can he do this to me?

Sally rang the back door bell and came in.

"Hello, Anne, it's me," she called.

"I'm in here," Anne called from the utility room where she was putting clothes in the dryer.

"How are you?" Sally asked.

"I could bite spoons in half," Anne said.

"What's the matter?"

"Hugh's home, and I don't know if I'm coming or going. I'm glad he's here. I think it's good. I'm glad we're having a new start. But I'm mad at myself for making a fuss over him. Here I am cleaning house as though my mother had come, and it's only Hugh, this bum I married who ran off with another woman. I don't know whether to hug him or kick him in the nuts!"

Sally laughed. "Oh, Anne. It's so funny! This is not like you. You're rushing off in two directions at once."

"Well, I don't think it's so funny. It doesn't feel funny. I want it to feel good, and it does sometimes, but then I'm angry again."

"I think you're going to make it. I'd feel the same way if Ken had done what Hugh did. Don't you think you'll get over this?"

"I hope so. I'm ready for things to settle down again. How does this sound for supper tonight? I could have shrimp creole with rice, asparagus, jelled fruit salad, French bread, and pound cake with strawberries for desert."

Sally laughed again. "I can't believe you, Anne! One minute you're ready to run him through the food processor and the next minute you're treating him like a guest of honor. Why don't you just have hamburgers and let him cook them on the grill?"

"You think that would be better?"

"Sure, keep it simple and let him do his part."

"Maybe that would be better. Oh, damn, Sally. I don't know what I'm doing."

"Just relax. It's going to be okay. Give yourself some time. Let him exert some effort, too. It's going to take both of you to make it, you know."

"You're right. I just want so much for everything to work out all right. I'm trying too hard. How about a cup of coffee?"

"Sounds good."

Anne took out two mugs.

"Where's Hugh now?" Sally asked.

"He's found a new job. He had applied at Venture Equities and they made him an offer. He's going to be an options trader for them."

"That sounds really good, Anne. I hope everything goes well for him and for you."

"I hope so, too. I think we can make it. I know I'm willing to work at it, and I just hope Hugh is, too. I think he is."

"It probably won't be easy."

"I realize that, but it's worth working for."

"You know, Anne, you're great for forgiving Hugh and trying to go on with the marriage."

"You think so? I'm just trying to make the best of it. I certainly don't feel heroic, and if Hugh takes off again, I'll kill him!"

"It's also pretty amazing that Hugh has come around. I didn't think he could do it," Sally said.

"Yea. The fact that he's been willing to go for counseling has made all the difference."

"You think he's pretty terrific, don't you?"

"Yes. In a way."

"Love conquers all," Sally said.

Hugh pulled open the glass door and entered the lobby of the Bank of America building in Charlotte. He pushed the elevator button for the 29th floor and rode to the plush offices of Venture Equities. His own office looked bare--he hadn't moved in his books, framed prints and mementoes yet--but well equipped and functional. The day was early, and he began making phone calls to touch base with the options people he would be dealing with through the day.

Then, before the financial markets opened, he called Fort Lauderdale, first to the real estate agent who had sold him his condominium, then to the Cigarette boat dealer, and arranged for both to begin the process of selling the big-ticket items he had purchased from them only a few months before. He would keep the Corvette and go down to pick it up as soon as he could.

He hoped he would not lose too much money on the sales. He had mixed feelings about unloading them. He felt good to be getting rid of the residue of an unhappily-driven period in his life, but sad to be giving up his dream. So much for Fort Lauderdale.

In his cell phone contacts, he noticed Margo's name and number. He deleted it.

The voice of the receptionist came over his intercom, "Your brother is here to see you."

"Send him back," Hugh said.

Hugh went out into the hall to greet Dave.

"How good to see you," he said.

"I just came by to see how you're doing in your new setting," Dave said. "These offices are really nice."

"Yea, somebody did a good job of designing them," Hugh said, taking Dave into his office and showing him a chair while he sat behind the desk.

"So, how's it going?" Dave said.

"I'm finding my way around here," Hugh said. "Haven't made anybody much money yet, but I will."

"How is Anne doing?"

"I think she's doing all right. She seems upbeat."

"She's been through a lot."

"I know."

"How are you feeling?"

"I'm feeling good, much better than I ever thought I would. I still feel guilty sometimes, and I don't have those soaring highs like I used to, but I haven't been depressed, either. It's different. There's not as much excitement, but there are not as many problems. And I seem to be able to work hard and concentrate well."

"I'm glad you've done so well. Not many men can let go of their macho enough to get help. Most just dig their heels in and won't admit that anything needs changing or that they've done anything wrong. Men have to ask if they want their marriage or their pride. The marriage is better."

"Well, all I know is I didn't want my life to be like Dad's. I think he was miserable before he died. The alcohol was his attempt at a cure, but it didn't work very well. I can't know for sure if Dad committed suicide, but I have a strong feeling that he did. And if he did, his life must have been pretty awful for him to have wanted to do that. I kept thinking, there must be some other way. I'd rather try the lithium than do things the way he did."

"I think you're wise."

"We'll see how it works out. So far, so good."

Hugh stood in the living room alone, gazing out the window without seeing, feeling tense. Evening was approaching, soon it would be dark. Anne was in the kitchen fixing supper, and the girls were in the den. The tension Hugh felt discomfited him. Anne was trying hard to make things work, and he was trying too. The innocent honesty of the girls, though, intensified his feeling of being out of place. His past absence hung over them like an unanswered question. Angie's naive inquiries haunted him. She had asked, "Are you going to stay with us now, Daddy?" when he was moving his clothes back into the closet.

"Of course I am," he had answered. He would rather have said, "We'll have to see," but he couldn't express that uncertainty to Angie. Angie had squealed delightedly and run off down the hall. Elizabeth, older, was more difficult to convince. She had learned that words don't always match actions, and Hugh sensed that she was waiting for proof.

He stood at the window, hoping he could erase his long absence from their memories. He was feeling on guard, and wished the family's attention would be focused on something other than the fact of his presence. He searched for ways to reduce the unhappy grip of the tension they were all feeling. He felt the disjointedness of his family, and sought ways to smooth it over.

Then, standing there, he hit upon the idea of the swimming pool. He would have a swimming pool built in the back yard. It would be a large, curvy pool with a sliding board for the girls and a diving board for adults. It would be set in a bright, tile patio, surrounded by tables with glass tops and blue umbrellas. Hugh envisioned this masterpiece, cool and blue like topaz, drawing his family together beside the protective mass of their splendid brick house. He would build a fence around the yard to ensure privacy, and plant white pines along it to soften its barrier.

He could picture himself, sitting at a table, drinking gin and tonic, reading Fortune Magazine, while Angie and Elizabeth splashed at the slide and Anne brought them all snacks. He would dive into the pool and swim its length underwater, savoring the unaccusing silence of its depths, reveling in its peace, bathed in the sensuous flow of water over his body, cleansing away the scabs of the past.

The pool would bring it all together--family, fortune, future, in a great baptism of its flashing blue, living waters. It would dwell there beside the house, calling the children in the hot summer afternoons, beckoning Anne with leisure, drawing him to its coolness after work, and at night, standing glassy-surfaced in the dark, catching fallen stars and flinging them heavenward again.

Hugh latched onto his pool as an idea that brought wholeness out of brokenness, and he went for it with great energy.

"A swimming pool! Daddy's gonna build a swimming pool!" Angie had squealed when Hugh told her.

"What's this all about?" Anne asked.

"I want to build a swimming pool in the back yard," Hugh said. "I thought it would be nice to have, and the kids can invite their friends over."

"Where are you going to put it?"

"Right up next to the house, just outside the den. We can build a big patio around it, and cover the part near the house with a sun roof. It would look like this," Hugh said, and drew a sketch on a kitchen napkin.

"Do you think we really need this right now?" Anne asked.

"Sure. We've got to go forward," Hugh said.

"But you've just moved back in. I'd like us to spend some time working on our relationship first."

"We'll do that. This won't interfere with that."

"I don't know, Hugh. It's going to be a mess when they start digging up the yard. We'll have red clay everywhere and workmen here all day."

"It won't take them that long. They can build these things in a month. Just think how nice it will be to jump into on a hot summer afternoon. And we can have parties out there."

"But just think how much time we'll have to spend taking care of it," Anne said. "Do you know what you have to do to keep one of those things clean and keep the chemicals right?"

"Ah, we'll handle that. That won't be any big problem."

"Well, don't expect me to maintain it."

"The kids and I can do that."

"Are we gonna get a swimming pool?" Elizabeth burst into the kitchen, excited.

"Yep," Hugh said, while Anne said simultaneously, "We're just thinking about it."

"Oh, wow!" Elizabeth said. "When?"

"As soon as we can get things started," Hugh said. "It will probably be ready by spring."

"All right!" Elizabeth said. "That'll be fun."

"Gimmie five," Hugh said, and Elizabeth slapped his hand with hers, then ran back out of the room.

"Wait a minute, Hugh. You're acting like this has already been decided."

"Well, why not? It would be nice, and we can afford it. I'm selling the boat and the condominium, so we can use some of that money for the pool."

"Great, but what if I don't want it!"

"Oh, you'll like it. And you see how excited the girls are about it."

"I know, Hugh, but I just don't think we need all this right now."

"Look, it won't hurt anything, and we'll enjoy it."

"Well, in the future, I'd like to be consulted before you make decisions for the whole family."

"Oh, come on Anne, it'll be good for us. We need something like this to cheer us up. It'll give us something to look forward to. We've all been through a lot."

"And we're not finished with it yet. We've got a lot of work to do on our relationship."

"I know, but that will come."

"Not if we ignore it."

"We'll get there. Don't worry. Now, come along with this pool idea. It'll help us."

Anne thought for a moment, looking down at the kitchen floor. "Hugh, no! We are not building a pool. We will join the neighborhood pool."

Hugh was startled. He wasn't used to having anyone contradict him. But he owed it to Anne. "Okay. That's a good plan."

Stirred, Anne left for the grocery store. She pushed her grocery cart along the aisles of the supermarket, picking up a dozen items on her list. She passed the canned meats, came to the soups and stopped in front of them looking for bisque of tomato. She began to feel calmer. We'll work these conflicts out, she thought. It's all part of the process. At least Hugh's home, so maybe there's hope. Her mind flashed back over the long months of pain, the months of wondering where Hugh was and who he was with. She felt that pain and anger again.

She found the bisque of tomato and put two cans in the cart. Then, just as she was turning to move on, Marilyn Arrington came around the corner.

"Well, hello, Anne. How are you?" Marilyn said in her husky voice.

"Hey, Marilyn," Anne said, surprised at the intrusion into her thoughts. "It's been a long time since I've seen you."

"It has been a long time, hasn't it? But how are you doing?"

"I'm doing okay. Hugh is back and we're trying to make a go of it."

"Sally told me you were back together. I just hope you don't get hurt again, Anne."

"I hope not too," Anne said, a twinge of depression passing through her.

"I guess it's worth a try," Marilyn said.

"Yes. I have to try. But how are you, Marilyn?"

"Oh, just ducky. Trot has remarried, and his new wife is a bitch who hates us. She's trying to get Trot to cut down on the child-support payments. I've got my lawyer defending us. He cuts down and I'll stick it to him in court. That bitch'll learn what she's got to live with."

"This fighting must be awful."

"Sure, but you get used to it. When you marry a bastard, you pay the price. Life is great if you can stand up to it."

Marilyn adjusted the bread in her cart so it wouldn't get crushed.

"You know something, Anne?" she said, changing her tone. "You sure are lucky."

"What?" Anne said.

"You're lucky, Anne," Marilyn said. "In this upside-down world, you're real lucky." She started to cry and walked quickly away, pushing her grocery cart. Anne's eyes followed her. Then Anne turned and went slowly up the aisle behind her, lost in thought. She came out of it in the frozen food section when some cartons of moose tracks ice cream--Hugh's favorite--caught her eye. She studied them, deciding. Then she put two in her cart and headed for the check-out counter and home.

That evening, after supper, Anne walked to the neighborhood pool, just to check it out. The gate was unlocked. The pool was furnished with comfortable lounge chairs. The pool deck was very clean and smelled fresh, like chlorine. Anne walked to the side of the pool and looked at the glassy water undulating softly. Then she saw them. Tiny points of light reflected in the pool. Stars. Their light came from deep in space, to that very pool. Their light bounced off the surface and glinted back into the heavens. Anne lingered a moment, thinking about this. Then she turned on her heel, faced the uncertain darkness, and walked home.

THE END

Made in the USA
Middletown, DE
25 October 2024